Shema Bekolah: The High Holiday Collection

Edited by Jofa

Shema Bekolah: The High Holiday Collection

2023 Paperback Edition, *First Printing*
© 2023 by Jofa: Jewish Orthodox Feminist Alliance

ISBN: 9798859410316

Shema Bekolah:
The High Holiday Collection
CONTENTS

3

4

YOM KIPPUR

SUKKOT/ SIMCHAT TORAH

INTRODUCTION

Daphne Lazar Price

וַיֹּאמֶר הֹ' אֶל־אַבְרָהָם...
כֹּל אֲשֶׁר תֹּאמַר אֵלֶיךָ שָׂרָה שְׁמַע בְּקֹלָהּ...
But God said to Abraham...
whatever Sarah tells you,
listen to her voice...
~Genesis 21:12

The passage containing the phrase *"shema bekolah"* appears in Genesis 21 in a setting that is troubling to our modern-day sensitivities. Sarah demands that Abraham cast out Hagar and her son. Abraham is distressed by this request, and is likely about to deny Sarah, until God intervenes and tells him *"shema bekolah"* – whatever Sarah tells you, do as she says. This phrase has inspired dozens upon dozens of women to write for Jofa's *Shema Bekolah* series of *Divrei Torah*, consisting of researched commentary and personal reflections about Jewish holidays throughout the year. This *Shema Bekolah: The High Holiday Collection* compilation draws on both new and previously published pieces.

Women have been ever-present in Jewish narratives, from the creation story to the formation of Jewish peoplehood, to telling of the Israelites' redemption, Talmudic and Midrashic tales, and beyond. Their presence and their voices are an integral part of Jewish tradition. Although women are present across Jewish texts, their commentaries on those texts have been missing from the communal Torah discourse at the heart of Orthodox life. And as girls' and women's learning has steadily increased, they have continually sought to share their learning through the spoken and written word.

Throughout the years, Jofa has prioritized elevating and amplifying women's scholarship, including supporting the publication of the *Shema Bekolah* articles written by women. The result has been a demonstration of the growth of women's learning. We are proud to share *Shema Bekolah: The High Holiday Collection*, a compendium of *Divrei Torah*. Publishing this collection is a natural outgrowth of Jofa's work. We are excited to produce this volume of Orthodox women's Torah commentary to add to institutions' and individuals' libraries.

There are many people to thank for the production of this book. First and foremost are the dozens of contributors to this book. When we put out the call for articles, women ranging from rabbis and spiritual leaders to academics to lay leaders from around the world responded with great enthusiasm. Second, nothing gets done at Jofa without the staff, Dr. Sarah Kranz-Ciment and Wendy Lefko Messeloff. Every day, they show up with their fullest selves to help advance the cause of Orthodox feminism. I am also grateful to Jofa's board chair, Dr. Mindy Feldman Hecht, and the members of Jofa's board for their dedicated leadership in all the big and little ways. Finally, this book could not have come to fruition without the help of Rabbi Menachem Creditor, who did not ask for credit but who will receive it anyway.

Chazak chazak v'nitchazek. May we all continue to grow both individually and collectively from strength to strength.

Selihot

The Spirituality of Intimacy: Thoughts on Selihot

Rabbi Dr. Erin Leib Smokler
Edited by Ronda Arking

(previously published on Jofa.org)

The selihot service, which we are soon to recite, is a mysterious one. The time of prayer is unusual, the liturgy is opaque, and the overall structure of it has the quality of a tribal chant. Over and over we repeat certain phrases, returning to them again and again, building momentum as the mantra continues through the night and then through the season.

> "ה' ה' א-ל רחום וחנון," we intone, "The Lord, the Lord, a compassionate and gracious God."

What is the meaning of it all? Why the stirring repetition? Why was the selihot service constructed in this way, with every single poem followed by its own recitation of the thirteen attributes of God's mercy—

> ויעבר ה' על פניו ויקרא :ה' ה' אל רחום וחנון ארך
> אפים ורב חסד ואמת נצר חסד לאלפים נשא עון
> ופשע וחטאה ונקה
>
> And the Lord passed before [Moshe] and proclaimed: The Lord, the Lord! A compassionate and gracious God, slow to anger, and abounding in kindness and truth, keeping kindness for the thousandth generation, forgiving of iniquity, willful sin, and error, and cleansing...

These words have echoed through generations of penitents.

11

A fantastical tale in the Gemara seems to lie at the heart of this practice. We learn in Talmud Bavli, Tractate Rosh Hashana 17b:

ויעבר ה 'על פניו ויקרא :אמר רבי יוחנן :אלמלא
מקרא כתוב אי אפשר לאומרו .מלמד שנתעטף
הקדוש ברוך הוא כשליח צבור ,והראה לו למשה
סדר תפלה .אמר לו :כל זמן שישראל חוטאין יעשו
לפני כסדר הזה ואני מוחל להם.

The Lord passed before [Moshe] and proclaimed. Rabbi Yohanan said: If this Scriptural verse had not been written, it would be impossible to say it! It teaches that the Holy One, Blessed be He, wrapped Himself [in a tallit] like a leader of prayer, and said to Moshe: Whenever the Jews sin before Me, let them perform this procedure and I shall forgive them.

The passage later continues:

אמר רבי יהודה :ברית כרותה לשלש עשרה מדות
שאינן חוזרות ריקם ,שנאמר (שמות לד)הנה אנכי
כרת ברית.

Rabbi Yehudah said: A covenant was made regarding the thirteen attributes, that they would never return empty — that is, that they would never be ineffective in bringing about God's favor — as it says [in Shemot 34], I hereby make a covenant.

It seems that according to Rabbi Yohanan and Rabbi Yehudah, the thirteen attributes really do have mystical powers. Moshe was taught by God at Sinai a formula for forgiveness that was then sealed in a covenant for all time. The prescription for divine exoneration would lie in a verbal incantation that would not fail. Declaring God's merciful goodness would always yield such goodness.

When the master gives one the key to his own appeasement it behooves one to listen.

The rabbis who authored the selihot—mostly geonim and rishonim who lived from the eighth through the fifteenth centuries—did just that. They inserted the incantation repeatedly into the service, performing the procedure exactly according to the rules. Their fealty to this Gemara is signaled in the liturgy that they composed. Just before we recite the attributes, we recapitulate Rosh Hashana 17b, saying:

אל הורית לנו לומר שלש עשרה, וזכור לנו היום
ברית שלש עשרה, כמו שהודעת לענו מקדם

O God, you taught us to recite the Thirteen [attributes of mercy], so remember for us today the covenant of these Thirteen, as you made known to the humble one [i.e., Moshe] in ancient times...

Yet confusion still remains. What is left out of the Gemara, as well as this restatement of it, is: Why? Why do these specific words effectuate divine forgiveness? What about them makes them consummate vehicles for teshuvah, for the human return to God and the Godly return to humanity? What is the magic of the formula?

I submit to you that the essence of the Thirteen is not to be found in rote recitation, but in contextual examination. We must return to the part of the Torah in which these words were revealed if we are to understand their transformative power.

This grand forgiving encounter between God and Moshe is found originally in Shemot 34: 5-7, in parshat Ki-Tissa. There, Moshe received the first set of tablets, smashed the first set of tablets, and punished the people for their egregious sin of the golden calf that took place in the interim. When we meet Moshe again in chapter 34, verse 1, God has just commanded him to carve the second tablets and to await God's presence on Mount Sinai.

ויאמר ה' אל משה פסל לך שני לחת אבנים
כראשונים וכתבתי על הלחת את הדברים אשר
היו על הלחת הראשונים אשר שברת.

And the Lord said to Moshe, carve you two stone tablets like the first ones, and I shall write on the tablets the words that were on the first tablets, which you shattered.

Moshe complies in 34:4:

ויפסל שני לחת אבנים כראשונים וישכם משה
בבקר ויעל אל הר סיני כאשר צוה ה' אותו ויקח
בידו שני לחת אבנים.

And he carved two stone tablets like the first ones, and Moshe rose early in the morning and went up to Mount Sinai as the Lord had charged him, and he took in his hand the two stone tablets.

The immediate result brings God to Moshe and us to our now familiar verses, in Shemot 34:5-6:

(5) וירד ה' בענן ויתיצב עמו שם ויקרא בשם ה'
(6) ויעבר ה' על פניו ויקרא: ה' ה' אל רחום וחנון
ארך אפים ורב חסד ואמת.

(5) And the Lord came down in the cloud and stood with him there and proclaimed the name of the Lord.
(6) And the Lord passed before him and called out: The Lord, the Lord! A compassionate and gracious God, slow to anger, and abounding in kindness and truth.

Notice the pairing of these sentences. Rabbi Yohanan, in the Gemara, commenting on the words, "And the Lord passed before him and called out," began the "forgiveness formula" there, with verse 6. But the composers of the selihot deviated from the formula! They took us one verse back, to a critical, intimate, profound moment between God and Moshe, in 34:5. "וירד ה' בענן" — "God descended from on high to get close to Moshe. This was not to be a revelation through thunder and lightning, fear and trembling. This revelation, this second matan torah of the second tablets, was to be the revelation of intimacy, of God coming down to humanity softly, quietly, lovingly. "ויתיצב עמו שם" — God stood with Moshe, united in solidarity and shared purpose, mutuality and reciprocity. Only a few verses back, in 33:21, God had indicated that there was such a possibility, such a place of seamless closeness.

"הנה מקום אתי ונצבת על הצור" – "There is a place with Me" — said God to Moshe. "Stand on the rock." In our verse, we find the fulfillment of that vision in "ויתיצב עמו שם", only now both Moshe and God stand on the rock of Sinai, fortified in their togetherness.

In choosing to add this one verse to Rabbi Yohanan's prescription, the selihot writers opened up a whole new meaning for teshuvah. Teshuvah, repentance, is not about words or pre-written formulas, but about the pursuit of a certain kind of relationship. The thirteen attributes are not a magical recipe for forgiveness, but rather signifiers of a different kind of relationship with God, one most conducive to compassion. In the process of teshuvah, the constant refrain teaches us, we ought to be striving for a spirituality of intimacy wherein God's presence is real and we are fully present. This is the task of real return: The relationship of "ויתיצב שם עמו"—"of standing side by side with God because we make ourselves worthy and open to such an encounter.

How do we get there? God tells us this, too: "פְּסָל לְךָ שְׁנֵי לֻחֹת אֲבָנִים כָּרִאשֹׁנִים," Carve the stone and I will write upon it (34:1 Shemot). You do the work. You take the initiative. You assume responsibility. Then, says God, I will join you. The second tablets, alas, were not like the first, which were miraculously handed to Moshe from the heavens. The second tablets were earthly, human. They came from a fallible, flawed world. Moshe brought them to the mountain, not from the mountain. And yet, these second tablets were the tablets that endured. These second tablets of partnership, of human exertion met by divine sanction—these would stand the test of time. And even more than that, they would forever symbolize the greatest of all possibilities: the possibility of a second chance.

Ultimately, the transformative power of selihot and of the upcoming holidays of Rosh Hashana and Yom Kippur lies in this very message. Forgiveness is real; second beginnings, second revelations, and second selves are attainable. We just need to carve out a little bit of space within ourselves for God to write upon us.

We are told in the Gemara (Taanit 30b) that there were no celebrations in ancient Israel like those on Yom Kippur, for on that day the second tablets were given. Of course such an occasion calls for celebration, we now understand—the celebration of all that we might yet be.

As we enter into the depths of teshuvah during this time, as we cry out "ה' ה' אֵל רַחוּם וְחַנּוּן," let us remember to revel in the awesome responsibilities and awesome possibilities that lay before us. Let us work hard, so that God might too, and so that we might merit to stand together with God.

Selichot: Communal Return Through Personal Introspection

Rabbi Dina Najman

(previously published on Jofa.org)

Since the month of Elul began, we have been listening to the shofar blast and reciting Psalm 27, לְדָוִד ה אוֹרִי וְיִשְׁעִי מִמִּי אִירָא "Of David, God is my light and my salvation..." twice daily. As we begin to recite Selichot (penitential prayers), we feel a sense of trepidation and fear. Did we utilize the previous weeks as a time of reflection to increase our good deeds and spiritual development? On Selichot night, one week before Rosh Hashana, each of us asks: How will I stand before God on yom hadin, the Day of Judgment? In fact, the structure of the Selichot service prepares us for this awesome encounter.

The organizers of the Selichot service structured it with a brief שֶׁבַח (praise) section, a substantial בַּקְשָׁה (request) section and then a brief section of הוֹדיה, (thanksgiving) offered at the conclusion of the service. The service is anchored by the extensive liturgy of the בַּקְשָׁה section in which we ask God to forgive us, to remember us and to bestow mercy upon us.

It is interesting to note which prayer was chosen to inaugurate the בַּקְשָׁה section. Every day, whether the Selichot are long, as on Erev Rosh Hashana, or short as on Erev Yom Kippur, the first בַּקְשָׁה recited is:

17

לְךָ אֲדֹנָי הַצְּדָקָה וְלָנוּ בֹּשֶׁת הַפָּנִים. מַה־נִּתְאוֹנֵן וּמַה־נֹּאמַר. מַה־נְּדַבֵּר וּמַה
נִּצְטַדָּק: נַחְפְּשָׂה דְרָכֵינוּ וְנַחְקֹרָה וְנָשׁוּבָה אֵלֶיךָ. כִּי יְמִינְךָ פְּשׁוּטָה לְקַבֵּל שָׁבִים
לֹא־בְחֶסֶד וְלֹא־בְמַעֲשִׂים בָּאנוּ לְפָנֶיךָ. כְּדַלִּים וּכְרָשִׁים דָּפַקְנוּ דְלָתֶיךָ: דְּלָתֶיךָ
דָּפַקְנוּ רַחוּם וְחַנּוּן. נָא אַל־תְּשִׁיבֵנוּ רֵיקָם מִלְּפָנֶיךָ: מִלְּפָנֶיךָ מַלְכֵּנוּ רֵיקָם אַל־
תְּשִׁיבֵנוּ. כִּי אַתָּה שׁוֹמֵעַ תְּפִלָּה:

What can we speak? And how can we justify ourselves?
Let us search into our ways and examine them, and
return to You; for Your right hand is extended to receive
those who repent. Neither with virtue nor with good
deeds do we come before You, but like the poor and
needy, we knock at Your door. Please do not turn us
away empty handed from Your Presence, for You hear
[our] prayers.

Why was this prayer, written by Rav Amram Gaon in the
9th century, chosen as the first prayer of בַּקָּשָׁה? Why not
begin with the 13 "Attributes of Mercy," which Moshe
recited after the sin of the golden calf? On the verse
introducing these 13 Attributes , Va'ya'avor Hashem al
Panav –"God passed before Moshe and proclaimed, our
Sages comment in the Babylonian Talmud (Rosh Hashana
17b) that God was presented like a shli'ach tzibur (prayer
leader). God showed Moshe the proper procedure for
prayer telling him, "Whenever the Children of Israel sin,
they shall perform before Me this procedure and I will
forgive them." Therefore, it would seem that we should
begin the requests of the Selichot service by reciting the 13
Attributes, since God has told us to articulate this formula
to elicit Divine forgiveness.

Moreover, why not begin by affirming the brit (Covenant)
between God and the Jewish people? Shouldn't we begin
our requests by mentioning the brit, which connects God
to the people of Israel? Instead, we begin by stating that
we are inadequate and unworthy of God's forgiveness. We
beg for God's mercy while admitting that we lack virtue
and are spiritually incomplete.

Throughout the year, we attempt to present ourselves to others and to ourselves as individuals connected to our faith and committed to God. Even if we have theological struggles, we endeavor to observe the commandments and attempt to deepen our closeness to God. Haven't we then succeeded in some measure this past year by continuing to identify ourselves as attentive and committed to God's commandments? And yet, even if we are righteous, we do not come before God with our righteous deeds. As we say in the conclusion of the Selichot service:

כִּי לֹא עַל צִדְקֹתֵינוּ אֲנַחְנוּ מַפִּילִים תַּחֲנוּנֵינוּ לְפָנֶיךָ כִּי עַל רַחֲמֶיךָ הָרַבִּים

For not because of our good deeds do we supplicate ourselves before You. Rather, [we can only appeal] to Your abundant mercy.

When we enter the Selichot period, we begin by casting ourselves as impoverished individuals. We do not take credit for our accomplishments. We acknowledge that it is God who provides the conditions, the influences and the circumstances which enable our achievements. Despite the Divine efforts on our behalf, we did not attain all that was possible. We did not live up to our potential.

This reflection on our misdeeds and shortcomings elicits a desire for teshuva (repentance), a return to the understanding and acknowledgment that a person is created in God's image. When we accomplish teshuva, we return to a self-concept that predates what we may have become through wrong choices and poor compromises. We return to a life of constant and conscious awareness of the Divine source. In this בַּקָּשָׁה, we declare: נחפשה דרכינו ונחקרה ונשובה אליך—"Let us search into our ways and examine them, and return to You." As chozrim b'teshuva (those who return through repentance), we are actually reconnecting with our true selves. In his Shabbat Shuva drasha (Parashat VaYeilech 5634), the Sfas Emes, Rabbi Yehudah Aryeh Leib Alter of Ger (the second Gerer Rebbe, 19th Century Poland) explains that "the essence of teshuva is not repenting of the sin itself; rather, a person must return to cling to his Divine source."

This is why we begin with lecha Hashem HaTzedaka v'Anachnu boshet hapanim, "Righteousness is Yours God..." This formulation is not simply an expression of humility. Rather, it is an acknowledgment that we have achieved less than we could have in our relationship with God. If we are capable of shame, then we still have some sense of what we could be, hence, of where we come from. If we were shameless, we would have no hope of reconnecting with God. With arduous self-examination, we can come to understand that this is not our true self, which was created b'tzelem Elokim, (in the image of God). It is only then that we can move forward in the process of renewal. The sincere evaluation of our commitment to the Brit enables an understanding of what we have rejected by our misdeeds. The teshuva process requires recognition that it was far better for the individual when there was a close connection with God (prior to transgressing) in order to appreciate what has now been lost. The prophet Hosea expresses this longing when he describes the Israelites' desire to return to their intimate relationship with God after their infidelity:

אֵלְכָה וְאָשׁוּבָה אֶל־אִישִׁי הָרִאשׁוֹן כִּי טוֹב לִי אָז מֵעָתָּה׃
I will go and I will return to my first husband for it was better for me then than now. (Hosea 2:9)

Encouragement for this return can be found in the haftarah which precedes Selichot. Taken from the Book of

Isaiah, the Shabbat morning haftarah is the last of the seven haftarot of comfort following Tisha B'Av as well as the prelude to Selichot. This haftarah describes both the repair of our relationship with God and the potential for a new beginning.

In the haftarah, the prophet Isaiah in 62:5 proclaims,

וּמְשׂוֹשׂ חָתָן֙ עַל־כַּלָּ֔ה יָשִׂ֥ישׂ עָלַ֖יִךְ אֱלֹהָֽיִךְ׃

As a bridegroom rejoices over his bride, so will your God rejoice over you.

The rejoicing of a bridegroom over his bride is the deepest form of rejoicing possible. It is the beginning of the most intimate relationship between two people. An expression of this relationship is the well-known acronym for Elul, taken from the Song of Songs (6:3):

אֲנִ֤י לְדוֹדִי֙ וְדוֹדִ֣י לִ֔י

I am for my Beloved and my Beloved is for me...

We are reminded in Elul of our bond with God while simultaneously acknowledging that we have been unfaithful.

As members of Am Yisrael, our individual failings affect not only our personal relationship with God but the communal relationship with God as well. These two simultaneous relationships are interdependent. A rupture in an individual's relationship with God distances the people of Israel from God. Similarly, personal teshuva enables both the individual and the community to repair their relationship with God. Our personal teshuva becomes preparation for our communal teshuva. This is reflected in the Selichot liturgy. While lecha Hashem HaTzedaka v'Anachnu boshet hapanim may be recited in

21

individual prayer, the 13 Attributes, the community's prayer, must be recited in the presence of a minyan. These personal and communal elements of the Brit between God and the Jewish people are explicitly expressed in Nitzavim and Vayelech, the weekly Torah portions preceding Selichot.

As the children of Israel stand on the bank of the Jordan River, God renews the Brit with them:

אַתֶּם נִצָּבִים הַיּוֹם כֻּלְּכֶם לִפְנֵי יְהֹוָה אֱלֹהֵיכֶם
רָאשֵׁיכֶם שִׁבְטֵיכֶם זִקְנֵיכֶם וְשֹׁטְרֵיכֶם כֹּל אִישׁ יִשְׂרָאֵל:
טַפְּכֶם נְשֵׁיכֶם וְגֵרְךָ אֲשֶׁר בְּקֶרֶב מַחֲנֶיךָ מֵחֹטֵב עֵצֶיךָ עַד שֹׁאֵב מֵימֶיךָ:
לְעָבְרְךָ בִּבְרִית יְהֹוָה אֱלֹהֶיךָ וּבְאָלָתוֹ אֲשֶׁר יְהֹוָה אֱלֹהֶיךָ כֹּרֵת עִמְּךָ הַיּוֹם:

You stand this day, all of you, before the Lord your God: your heads, your tribes, your elders, and your officers, every man of Israel; your children, your wives and the stranger that is in the midst of your camp, from the hewer of your wood unto the drawer of water; that you should enter into the covenant of the Lord your God– and into God's oath–which the Lord your God makes with you this day. (Deuteronomy 29:9-11)

This Brit binds both the nation as a whole as well as its individual members. In these verses the people are referred to collectively as כֻּלְּכֶם (all of you), and then individually as כֹּל אִישׁ יִשְׂרָאֵל (every person of Israel). Every Jew, no matter what station, profession, or gender has a unique and personal connection with God. The yearning to return to a closer relationship with God begins our requests. From the opening paragraph Hashem HaTzedaka v'Anachnu boshet hapanim through the multiple repetitions of the 13 Attributes the community is propelled forward to the climactic moment of the Shema Koleinu – "Hear Our Voice." The ark is open, and we beseech God, Hashiveni Hashem eleicha –"Bring us back to You God and we shall return, renew our days like before."

The Selichot service positions us personally and as members of our community to return–as the Sfas Emes says–to our Divine source, and repair our relationship with God. We come prepared to stand before the Almighty on Yom HaDin – the Day of Judgement – to pray for the Divine mercy upon each individual, the nation of Israel and the Land of Israel.

May we all merit a healthy, happy and good life and a ketiva v'chatima tova.

Insights into the Month of Elul and the Tribe of Gad: A Time of Reflection, Courage and Change

Shoshanah Weiss

Elul is the time we start preparing for the high holy days of Rosh Hashana and Yom Kippur. The deep green leaves begin to transform into misty shades of yellow and maroon. The daylight become shorter and intense sunlight is waning. The cooler air flows and the winds and rain begin to increase. It is at this propitious time that we need to do internal reflection on our deeds and actions of the previous year. Elul is meant for soul reflection, growth, and courage to become a better Jew.

When we do an inventory of our actions and realize we need to change our ways we might become discouraged. Perhaps if we discover some deeper connections in Torah to the month of Elul, we can gain strength for our own unique abilities to deal with our task of self- improvement.

The great Kabbalist known as the Arizal or Rabbi Yitzchak Luria wrote in his sefer Yetzira that there is a connection between the months of the year and the 12 tribes of Israel. He connected Elul with the tribe of Gad. Both Yaakov Avinu and Moshe Rabenu gave blessings to the 12 tribes before they passed on to the next world. These blessings are intrinsic to gleaning the lessons of us in our inheritance as a nation.

In Moshe's blessing to the tribe of Gad, he praises them for their strength which resembled a lion. They were ferocious warriors and were fortunate to win the wars protecting Israel from their enemies. The tribe of Gad merited to inherit their land situated on the eastern bank of the Jordan river. This land had been ruled by the giants Sichon and Og. This special land was the first portion which was conquered even before they entered Eretz Yisrael. Part of their blessing from Moshe was that he blessed Gad to enlarge their boundaries. Rashi comments that Gad's portion had the ability to expand because, it wasn't in the area of Israel proper. It also states in Gemara Sotah 13b that Moshe Rabenu died in the portion of Reuven but was buried, in the portion of the tribe of Gad. No one knows according to the Talmud where Moshe's burial place is but we do know that the Gadites possessed a remarkable clarity and synthesis needed to teach the halachot of the Torah. This tribe was chosen by Moshe to be near his resting place in order to preserve the Torah and protect it with no break in the tradition. In addition, Gad's stone in the breast plate of the Kohein Gadol is an "achlamah" in Hebrew.[1] The Rabbi's derive out that this is an amethyst crystal and can strengthen the heart. It is interesting to note that this word can also spell the Hebrew word "milchamah", which means war in Hebrew. Another allusion to the warrior nature of the Gadites.

When Moshe Rabeinu died many Torah laws were lost. It states in Gemara Temura 16b that many years later after Moshe's death it was Osniel ben Kenaz, the first judge who is credited with retrieving many of these lost halachos.[2] Otniel was from the tribe of Gad. He was the main leader of the Jewish people after the death of Yehoshua.

Eliyahu Hanavi was also from the tribe of Gad and in the future will come to bring clarity and resolution to the debates in Talmudic discourse. He will also of course, usher in the era of Moshiach.

When we begin our process of reflection and personal growth during Elul it is important to gain strength from the characteristics of the tribe of Gad. We must be warriors in our mind and hearts to improve our ways. We must be steadfast in being loyal to the teachings of the Torah. Of course. it takes effort to make our own metamorphosis so that we can feel whole again at the time of heavenly judgement. Elul is a time to expand our opportunities for self- growth and refinement.

May we be blessed to work on our abilities to do teshuva as we enter the Rosh Hashana. May these efforts help us have more clarity into our lives and our goals for advancing our Torah learning. And may we merit to greet Eliyahu HaNavi , from the tribe of Gad, at the coming of the final redemption in our days!

Footnotes

1 Shivtei Yisrael by Rabbi Fishel Mael pg.349-357 (Shevet Gad)
2. ibid
3. ibid

Rosh Hashana

MEDITATION SCRIPT:
The Tekiah Container
for Our Brokenness
Rachel Anisfeld

(originally published at rachelanisfeld.com/2022/09/21/meditation-script-the-tekiah-container-for-our-brokenness-rosh-hashanah/)

Tekiah shevarim-teruah Tekiah.

The long steady Tekiah sounds of the shofar always surround the other more broken sounds of the shevarim and the teruah. In this meditation, we are going to consider the shevarim and teruah sounds to represent our brokenness and suffering, and the Tekiahs that stand on either side to represent the divine container that can hold all that brokenness and suffering.

We begin with the Tekiah, with a single long steady note. Hearing it in our mind –a single note held for a number of seconds, and feeling its steadiness, like the ground we walk on. One single steady note. No cracks, no holes. It is solid and secure. Taking some slow deep breaths and feeling this calm steadiness enter us. This is the steadiness of God inside us. Tekiah. Taking that in, breathing in the calm.

Into this space of steady security, we bring the shevarim-teruah. It is not just one kind of difficulty but multiple kinds – shevarim and teruah at once – brokenness, imperfection, failure, pain and difficulty of all sorts piled up inside us, so many different kinds, it is sometimes hard to see them separately, they get all nested together. Just feeling the whole piled up mess of suffering inside, allowing ourselves to touch it without really yet knowing what it all is.

Shevarim-teruah.

Hearing the broken notes, staccato like, first slower, then faster, and feeling the frenzy and the overwhelm that builds up, first slowly, then crazily inside. Confusion, overwhelm and shakiness.. Let yourself feel that energy in your body.

Tekiah again.

On either side of this shakiness and overwhelm, there stands a guard of steady calm. The shakiness is held inside this envelope, this container, this embrace, two strong arms holding a trembling, crying baby. See if you can feel the shaky energy and at the same time get a sense of its being held, that there is also something calm inside you that can hold the shakiness, no matter how shaky it becomes.

Really paying attention to the sense of a holding container, building your capacity to feel your own strength in this, to sense that It is you that is holding the shakiness, and at the same time that it is God in you, the solid steady presence of God in you. How do you sense that? Maybe it is through the breath, the sense of a cord of constant divine connection, the steady rhythm of your breath that breathes air all around the troubled places in your belly. Or maybe it is some steady place of rest in your heart, where God is always dwelling, the mishkan inside you. Or maybe it is your feet on the ground, feeling that solidness and letting it spread through your body, knowing that there is something that always holds you. Whatever it is, letting your sense of it strengthen. Tekiah. shevarim-teruah. Tekiah. On either side of the wobbliness is something solid. Sensing both the wobbliness and the strength of the container that can always hold it.

We practice. The shofar blows come again and again so that we can practice. After the initial sense of an overall pileup of difficulties inside – shevarim-teruah – we begin to untangle them and parse them out more slowly. Tekiah shevarim tekiah. We begin again with a Tekiah – the long steady slow sense of security. Maybe take a long slow breath, in and out, breathing deeply and letting that sense of calm steadiness return.

Shevarim.

And into that calm, this time we invite just shevarim, the first layer of brokenness inside us Not the most severe pain, the place of being totally shattered, but the slight nervousness, the cracks, that lie at the surface for us, maybe some gnawing worry or anxiety, some sense of not having met expectations, of failing in some way, some restlessness, or a feeling of irritation or anger.

Shevarim.

An initial taste of brokenness, of instability, of nervous energy. Touching all of that, and then Tekiah – bringing the calm back in to surround it, perhaps breathing again deeply to offer a calm container for the brokenness we just touched. It's ok. Practicing feeling the shevarim, the brokenness, the shakiness, and at the same time feeling the calm divine-human container inside us that can hold it.

And now we move deeper.

Tekiah teruah Tekiah.

Sensing first again the Tekiah container, the long steady note, the deep breath of calm that sends stillness through our bodies. And into that container, we invite teruah, a rasping, sputtering cry of shatteredness. Only go as deep as feels comfortable to you in this moment, becoming aware of the places inside us that hold the pain of our most shattered selves, of the places that we feel most broken and hurt, despairing and collapsed, the sense of unworthiness and not mattering, of nothingness, like an empty shell, a glass that has shattered into a thousand pieces and has no hope of repair. Just touching that sensation inside us with the heartbreaking sound of the teruah cry.

And holding that sensation of a deep existential shattering of the self, holding that in our Tekiah container so that it can rest in the steady unbroken calm of that secure embrace. Picture the shattered pieces of yourself, the thousand pieces of broken glass, and picture the solid Tekiahs on either side. These Tekiahs retain the memories of wholeness contained in all that shatteredness, they remember and know and believe and have confidence in the ultimate wholeness of all those shattered pieces, and in that knowing, the Tekiahs convey to the broken pieces that sense of wholeness, so that they can feel in themselves how they could be glued together, they can imagine it and see their own healing and repair and wholeness even as they are still shattered. The memory and faith in their wholeness holds them now in their brokenness. Or perhaps imagining the teruah again as a baby inside you crying desperately with flailing limbs and a pitiful broken cry, and seeing the two Tekiahs as your own two large hands of warm embrace that can hold your baby. They are both your hands and at the same time, God's hands, the energy of God's love running through you to hold them, the knowledge that comes from God of the calm and wholeness that underlies all the shattered pieces of you and of all creation.

This time as we come to the Tekiah, there is a new stillness and wholeness that comes to us. Tekiah Gedolah. Through our encounter with all this brokenness, we have actually come to some expanded stillness and wholeness. The space is bigger. It can hold more pain. The container is wider and more steady, the sense of wholeness more complete, the calm more secure.

That final Tekiah Gedolah is a call home to all the scattered, shattered, farflung parts of ourselves, wherever they are. אִם־יִהְיֶה נִדַּחֲךָ בִּקְצֵה הַשָּׁמָיִם מִשָּׁם יְקַבֶּצְךָ ה' אֱלֹקיךָ וּמִשָּׁם יִקָּחֶךָ: Even if your castouts are at the ends of the world, from there the Lord your God will gather you, from there He will fetch you.

Tekiah Gedolah.

Hear the long steady call – come hoooooome. And see them all, limping and stumbling and struggling in all their brokenness, but still coming, a new sense of hope washing over them, drawn inward to a center of calm and peace, to home, to healing, to wholeness. God is calling them home. Tekiah Gedolah. Come hoooome. Feel all the shattered pieces drawn together, like broken shards of glass coming together to re-form themselves into the glass jar they originally were, each one showing its beauty now, sparkling, flying into its place, forming a whole, a kaleidoscope of stunning brokenness and wholeness, all drawn home by the call – Tekiah Gedolah. Come hooome. God is calling you home.

Resting now in the quiet after the Tekiah Gedolah, in the reverberations of wholeness and stillness. Sitting very still and letting yourself rest in this sense of wholeness and stillness.

We do this again and again, go through these rounds, and maybe on each cycle we expand the circle to include more of the brokenness, more of the suffering, more of the scattered shards of ourselves, drawing more into the Tekiah container, making the space ever larger to hold whatever needs to be held. And over time, as we continue to hear the call, maybe we also expand the Tekiah container to include brokenness outside of ourselves as well. We will do one more short Tekiah cycle now. Spending a moment right now, if it feels right, bringing to mind some pieces of brokenness from outside you that you would like to draw into our expanded Tekiah container, perhaps the suffering of someone you care about or the suffering in the larger world right now, a particular issue that is really upsetting you, maybe also the suffering of other people in this room, whatever it is, inviting all that in, bringing in all the world's brokenness and allowing it to rest in our widened Tekiah container, in spaciousness, allowing it all to rest inside you in some greater knowledge of wholeness and calm, something that does not deny the suffering but is large enough and secure enough to hold it for this moment in faith and steadiness. Breathing deeply and letting all parts of you and all the brokenness you have brought in, letting them all feel the steadiness and wholeness of God running through you. Whatever it is, it can be held here. Tekiah. Breathing deeply. Shevarim teruah – feeling the energy of unsteady

34

shakiness and suffering, the sadness of it all. Tekiah. Breathing deeply again and holding it all in the calm steady divine container of your breath.

Finishing off our shofar practice with a final Tekiah Gedolah. Take an even longer, deeper breath and let the calm of that pervade you. Calling it all home to this resting place inside you. Arriving at some stillness. You are whole. You are at peace. Tekiah Gedolah. All the brokenness is held right here, in this divine-human container. Sensing how we built this Tekiah container together, each on our own, but also together, the strength of doing this in a group, right now and in our communities on Rosh Hashana. Resting for one more moment in your own Tekiah wholeness before letting go of the practice.

Listening to the Shofar Inside
Rachel Anisfeld

(Originally published on
https://rachelanisfeld.com/2022/09/22/quick-thought-listening-to-
the-shofar-inside-rosh-hashanah/)

The shofar speaks in a language that does not have words, is
beyond words. It is the soul's language, somehow mournful,
joyous, triumphant and pleading all at once, beyond time and
space, eternal, primordial and otherworldly. More powerful
than speech in its emotional intensity and impact, it is a mode
of communication that bypasses the mind and enters straight
into our hearts so that we feel its call viscerally with a
different kind of knowing that we cannot explain or
articulate. This is how God speaks to human beings.

There are places inside us that speak this shofar language
regularly, and they, too, are the voices of God, though we
recognize them not. They cry out without words to be heard,
vague sensations of yearning or unease or sadness or awe or
even an inkling of ethereal delight, sometimes loud,
sometimes softer, sometimes a sharp pang, like a tekiah, and
at other times, more of a throbbing sensation, like a shevarim,
or a sense of frenetic energy, like a teruah. We tend either to
dismiss them for their murkiness, to drown them out with
distraction, or to be so quick to analyze them and box them
into definition, causation and explanation that we suffocate
the vital life force they came to offer us. What they are asking
for is quiet patient attention, to sit in the dark with them and
let them unfold slowly, over the course of many hours and
one hundred cries – as with the shofar on Rosh Hashana – to
let their message remain misty and mystical and felt, and only
very slowly and gradually and tentatively to come into the
light of language and explicit understanding. They do want
to tell us something, but it is something that can only be

communicated subtly and slowly, so that realization dawns on us in its own sweet time.

This is how God speaks to human beings. We dismiss these messenger angels at our peril, and at the peril of the larger community that needs us to manifest as our fullest selves. When we learn to listen to them, when we begin to turn towards them instead of turning away, what we are doing is a very deep teshuva, a returning, both to ourselves and to the God who has been calling to us. The quiet, patient presence of our attending changes us; it softens us and gentles us, so that there is a new kindness, both inside and out, and the wordless voices that are speaking inside us, often banished pieces of ourselves, far-flung scattered exiles like the Jewish people themselves, these parts of us, once heard, can gradually be gathered and re-integrated, making us whole and unified once again.

This is where redemption happens, slowly, inside us. The shofar is the first herald of the messianic era. Its blasts sound at first like woeful cries, but over time, they are transformed into the music of joy and celebration and triumph. It is listening that redeems them. On Rosh Hashana, the mitzvah is lishmo'a, to listen, to listen to the shofar's wordless calls and to listen to its echoes, divine echoes, inside us and also inside those around us, to really listen and turn towards the murky, nameless, uncertain stirrings that have come, on angel's wings, to speak to us, to heal us, and to bring us home.

The Happiness of the Returning Guest

Ilana Bauman

From Rosh Chodesh Elul until the end of Sukkot, we add a special prayer into our daily tefillah. In fact, we say it twice a day. Colloquially known as "L'David," Psalm 27 of Tehillim puts us in a mindset of awe as we appreciate and acknowledge all that Hashem does for us. There is one line that seems to convey a contradictory message. In the words of King David, we ask Hashem:

> "שבתי בבית ה' כל ימי חיי ,לחזות בנועם ה' ולבקר בהיכלו"
> "Shivti B'veit Hashem Kol Yemei Chayay, Lachazot B'Noam Hashem U'Levaker B'Heichalo"--May I dwell in the House of Hashem (Beit HaMikdash) all the days of my life, see the pleasantness of Hashem and visit His Holy of Holies.

Why do we ask to both dwell in and visit the Beit HaMikdash? What does it mean to simultaneously be a permanent resident and a guest? The Lubavitcher Rebbe offers a beautiful insight to explain this contradiction. He embraces the contradiction, as it embodies a mindset worth striving for. Like a permanent resident, we have many constants in our lives that become regular and routine to us - we wake up, we daven, we go to school, we go home, we eat dinner, we visit with our family, and we go to bed, just to do it all again the next day. And while it is so easy to get caught up in the repetition, it is our responsibility to not become jaded. Says the Lubavitcher Rebbe, this line of Tehillim is telling us that we should view these regular parts of our lives through the eyes of a visitor, a transient guest, looking at each day with new, wide eyes. We get to have the mindset of a visitor who feels the excitement of experiencing something for the first time, even as we are dwellers in our routine experiences.

Year after year we celebrate the same holidays. We dip the apple in the honey, blow the shofar, daven in shul, build and decorate a sukkah, and shake the lulav and etrog. The celebration can easily become monotonous and routine. But we are commanded in the Torah:

"ושמחת בחגך והיית אך שמח"

"V'Samachta B'Chagecha V'Hayita Ach Sameach" You should be happy on your holiday (Sukkot), and you will surely be happy.

There are many ways of reading this line, and I would like to offer one perspective. The wording of this command makes the experience of the holiday seem subjective, focused on "you," and I think that is intentional. Being a dweller, celebrating the same holidays in the same ways every year, who has the mindset of a visitor, viewing the regularly occurring events as extraordinary and exciting, is going to look different for each of us. Each of us will achieve this common goal in a different way. It is up to you, the Torah is telling us, to find something that makes you happy, that brings you joy, that gives you excitement. And in that way, you will experience the happiness of the returning guest, making this yearly and routine holiday experience your own, filled with the excitement you choose to infuse it with.

Wishing y'all all a happy, healthy, and sweet New Year filled with excitement and joy! Chag Sameach and Moadim L'Simcha!

A Challah Story for Rosh Hashana

Tzipi Boroda

Rosh Hashana is the birthday of the world. This aspect of the High Holydays fills me with a type of regret that I never felt when I was younger.

The challah we eat is round like a cake or a circle which has a sense of the celebration now tinged for me with that sense of the inevitability; of coming back to an uncertain beginning.

Rosh Hashana is grand and regal and all dressed up. It has trumpets and fancy food and guests but it all leads me to a sense that we failed at the last time around-at least I did.

I think the round challah we eat throughout the Tishrei festivals is more reminiscent of the mound of Mount Sinai, more fitting for Shavuot.

Shavuot is when we reap the wheat harvest. This is where the Jewish people should have culminated the heights of their understanding, according to the Aleinu prayer, of being the ones "to fix the world under the Kingdom of God, referring of course to our mandate for Tikkun Olam.

In Pirkay D'Rabbi Eliezer, there is a story that all the creatures came before God at the beginning of creation to bow before their Creator. God requested to join them, to go forth together to "Robe God in majesty" (Psalm 93:1) for "There is no Sovereign without a people."

God recognized this partnership as, in the recitation of the Shabbat evening kiddush, we say that "...God sanctified the seventh day because on it God rested from all the work God created to be done." (Gen 2:3) This 'work to be done' is widely believed to infer a partnership between God and humanity in the project of creation and redemption.

The familiar story in Midrash Rabba on the first chapter of Genesis recounts God's decision to create the humans in arguments to and fro about the merits of this decision with the angels.

The angels pointed out human frailties and tendencies for meaningless waste, baseless hatred and short sighted indulgences-in pursuit of power or short term gain.

God saw all this. There was a flood remember. Free will is a tricky thing but the very people who are fraught with so many ways to trigger their own destruction can grow and evolve, are given the agency for overcoming and creating the network of support to raise children, to collaborate, build community, to lift up the world all the way to that summit of possibility.

But on Rosh Hashana we are back to the bottom of the next rung. This doesn't mean we haven't gotten anywhere. We can see that circle we drew in the challah as a spiral up or down. Rosh Hashana is a suspension of time to consider which way we are going.

History, in Judaism, time in fact, is not circular but rather it is linear. It has a goal and that can be seen in at the beginning of the book of Numbers when the whole community was encamped in peace around the mountain. Then came the mutinies. The catalogue of faithlessness threatened, after the whole history of the great investment of God and the faltering Jewish people, to destroy the whole project of a model community that was so close to being achieved. They couldn't hold it together.

If we reach another Tisha B'Av, we know there is still much to repair. But with the coming of 5784, there is a new chance for hope.

My conception is that from Rosh Hashana until Simchat Torah, when the new Torah cycle begins again, when the account of creation is again read, time is in a kind of suspended animation. This is much like Shabbat is to the week.

Time can be suspended in mindfulness. We park our daily work for careful examination and reflection to see if our lives are lining up to the existential value of our higher purpose.

Before the first seed had sprouted on the earth, God could see the possibility of the bountiful harvest we could bring at Shavuot. We can envision, beyond the brokenness and the heartache, the summit of time within our reach.

The phrase in Lecha Dodi, the Shabbat song sung as the sun sets on the previous week has it,

> "Towards the Sabbath let us go, you and I
> For it is the very source of the blessing,
> from the Head,
> from of old
> She was chosen
> Last to be created,
> Conceived at the very beginning."

Let that Challah be our compass and remind us of the softness in our hearts and the plasticity of our minds. We are headed for greatness.

May you be signed and sealed in the book of life.

Finding Love Again:
A Rosh Hashana and
Yom Kippur of Connection
(A reflection during the pandemic)

Ruthie Braffman Shulman
Edited by Ronda Arking

Like so much else, Rosh Hashana and Yom Kippur will look very different this year. To the extent they are held at all, minyanim (prayer services) will be marked by limited attendance, socially-distant seating, and temperature checks; instead of handshakes and hugs with old friends, we'll make do with waving from behind our masked faces – if we're fortunate enough to attend services at all. Not surprisingly, our internal experience of Rosh Hashana and Yom Kippur will be fundamentally different as well.

In most years, Rosh Hashana and Yom Kippur halt our everyday routine and remind us of humanity's place in the world and God's Reign, Malkeinu. Hearing the shofar's piercing blast shatter the shared silence in our synagogue's sanctuaries and feeling the deep solemnity of the packed sanctuary at the Kol Nidrei prayer, we're called upon to meditate on God's greatness.

How small we feel, standing before the divine Judge and pounding on our hearts before our Creator; we are nothing but k'chomer b'yad hayotzer, "like clay in the hands of the potter," before God.

This year, the reminder to recall God's greatness and humanity's smallness feels superfluous. Across the world, we have witnessed human frailty in ways not seen for generations, as the haunting words of the Ashkenazic prayer Unetane Tokef have become part of our everyday existence: "מי יחיה ומי ימות – Who shall live and who shall die, who in their time, and who by an early death."

Every day of these past few months has felt as reflective and humbling as our feelings on Rosh Hashana and Yom Kippur – and sometimes even as uncertain and helpless as our feelings on Tisha B'Av.

However, our liturgy and tradition do not view Rosh Hashana and Yom Kippur exclusively through the lens of God as our Sovereign. While our relationship with God as Monarch is still front and center, this year we can focus on God as Avinu – as children seeking the comfort and shelter of a loving parent. This year, with so much upheaval and pain in the world, we can seek solace in God's love and care, as even during the darkest days, God is "Gazing through the window and peering through the lattice" – מַשְׁגִּיחַ מִן־הַחַלֹּנוֹת מֵצִיץ מִן־הַחֲרַכִּים: (Song of Songs 2:9).

In a passage that beautifully captures this aspect of prayer and our relationship with God, Rav Solveitchik described a struggle to pray while his wife was sick in the hospital. He could not bring himself to talk to the Creator in the whitewashed public space of the hospital, surrounded by nurses and interns. Upon returning home, however, the Rav writes "I would rush to my room, fall to my knees, and pray fervently. God, in those moments, appeared not as the exalted, majestic King, but rather as a humble, close friend, brother, father; in such moments of black despair, He was not far from me; he was right there in the dark room; I felt His warm hand, kaviyachol, [as it were] on my shoulder, I hugged His knees, kaviyachol [as it were]."

While Malkeinu prayers of judgment may be experienced with a group or in public, Avinu prayer requires a personal and intimate encounter between the individual and God. Avinu prayer is creating a safe space to be vulnerable and meet God as the most real version of ourselves; our fears, desires, strengths, and failings all have an equal audience in this private moment with the Almighty.

The Mishnah in Avot 5:5 lists 10 miracles in the Mikdash (Temple). In the eighth miracle listed, the Mishnah describes the space of the Mikdash miraculously expanding to allow the throngs of people packed into the courtyard to prostrate themselves simultaneously during the Avodah (temple service). Rav Ovadia Mi'Bartenura, a fifteenth-century commentator, adds a subtle detail that transforms the miracle from a neat trick into a statement about the essence of Yom Kippur. The Bartenura explains that the Mikdash expanded enough so that every single person had their own four amot (cubits) to recite a personal viduy without others overhearing. The miracle was not about having space for elbows and feet and bowing more comfortably. The miracle was that each individual had a private moment to experience intimacy and closeness with God; to embrace God as Avinu.

The personal and quiet space with God of Yom Kippur has a precedent going back to the original practice of the holiday – the Avodah in the Beit HaMikdash. The Kohen Gadol entered the Kodesh HaKodashim (Holy of Holies) five times on Yom Kippur – the only times a person was ever allowed to walk into that space. One of the instances when the Kohen Gadol entered the Kodesh HaKodashim to perform part of the Avodah he offered the ketoret (incense), pouring the incense onto the burning coals and filling the Kodesh HaKodashim with smoke. During the ketoret, the Torah tells us, all other kohanim had to leave the building and wait in the Temple courtyard (Leviticus 16:17). At this special moment, the Kohen Gadol was absolutely alone with God, with everyone else outside the building and the billowing clouds of the ketoret, preventing the possibility of even seeing the Kohen Gadol.

This year, we can all be the Kohen Gadol. We can transform the private spaces of our living rooms and synagogues into a personal Kodesh HaKodashim. In a minyan, it may be difficult to truly let oneself feel the honesty and vulnerability of being alone with the Creator. With the world as we know it turned upside down, we can use the private space of Rosh Hashana and Yom Kippur to feel the intimacy and closeness with God as Avinu – a sacred space to be alone for an honest and open conversation. For so many, these past few months have been painful:

Non-essential medical treatments have been put on hold; patience has worn thin on the emotional roller coaster of crumbling educational plans; anxiety floods in on the cloud hovering over our economic future; fear for the health and safety of our loved ones is ever-present. This year, surrounded by tension, frayed tempers, and sadness, let us supplement the fear of judgment with a focus on the joy of connection; of knowing that God loves us unconditionally and is always ready to embrace us as a parent. This may be what the Mishnah is calling for when it states "There were no days as happy for the Jewish people as the fifteenth of Av and as Yom Kippur—לא היו ימים טובים לישראל כחמשה עשר באב וביום הכיפורים (Taanit 30b).

Perhaps we can take this further and not only try to find solace and intention in the difference of minyan this year, but in the overall approach to the Yamim Noraim as well. In our introspection during tefillot this year, let each of us realize, focus, and nurture on the aspects of Judaism that we love and invigorate us. In therapy, couples are sometimes asked, "How did you first fall in love with your partner?" This year, let us ask ourselves how we first fell in love with Judaism. Was it a moment of inspired Torah study? A special connection to certain acts of kindness or certain mitzvot? A sense of connection and passion during prayer? Just as repentance involves kabbalah al ha'atid – a commitment to the future – this year, let us seek out the parts of Judaism we enjoy most and embrace them.

Amidst all the dark swirling clouds around the world, may we be blessed to fill Rosh Hashana and Yom Kippur with inspiration and connection and emerge as joyous as the Kohen Gadol emerging from the Kodesh HaKodashim – beaming with the happiness and joy that comes from a loving encounter with God.

"As We Are Now" or
"The Power of Praying for Others"
Ranana Dine

The Torah reading for the first day of Rosh Hashana can feel out of place. On the second day we read the story of the Akedah with all of its terrible grandeur, its theological profundity - appropriate for the Days of Awe. On Yom Kippur we read about the rituals and sacrifices specific to that day - also a fitting reading. But the stories of Avraham, Sara, Avimelekh, and Hagar from the first day's portion feel smaller, more domestic. I was always taught that the ostensible reason we read this passage is because of God's remembering of Sara and the birth of Yitzchak, and indeed God's memory is a significant theme of Rosh Hashannah, particularly in the Musaf Amidah. But in the Torah reading the moment of God's remembering - "V'Adonai Pakad et Sara" - is just that, a moment, literally the first few words, easily lost in the series of narratives about Avraham's adventures.

But I think there is another narrative and another moment that can provide insight into today - into the power of prayer and the processes of teshuva. This is the story of Hagar and Yishmael in the desert. Hagar, Sara's handmaiden, Avraham's concubine, is an unlikely heroine for Rosh Hashana, but her actions might just be the most exemplary of how we, normal fallible humans, can experience redemption and the power of prayer.

To review: After the birth of Yitzchak, Sara asks Avraham to cast out Hagar and Yishmael who she now sees as a threat. Avraham, with some urging by God, agrees and sends the pair out into the desert with some meager provisions. Soon the food and water runs out. Let's look at the verses that describe what happens next:

וַתֵּ֜לֶךְ וַתֵּ֣שֶׁב לָ֗הּ מִנֶּ֙גֶד֙ הַרְחֵק֙ כִּמְטַחֲוֵ֣י קֶ֔שֶׁת כִּ֣י אָֽמְרָ֔ה אַל־אֶרְאֶ֖ה בְּמ֣וֹת הַיָּ֑לֶד
וַתֵּ֣שֶׁב מִנֶּ֔גֶד וַתִּשָּׂ֥א אֶת־קֹלָ֖הּ וַתֵּֽבְךְּ׃

And she [Hagar] went and sat down at a distance, a bowshot away; for she thought, "Let me not look on as the child dies." And sitting thus afar, she burst into tears.

וַיִּשְׁמַ֣ע אֱלֹהִים֮ אֶת־ק֣וֹל הַנַּעַר֒ וַיִּקְרָא֩ מַלְאַ֨ךְ אֱלֹהִ֤ים ׀ אֶל־הָגָר֙ מִן־הַשָּׁמַ֔יִם
וַיֹּ֥אמֶר לָ֖הּ מַה־לָּ֣ךְ הָגָ֑ר אַל־תִּ֣ירְאִ֔י כִּֽי־שָׁמַ֧ע אֱלֹהִ֛ים אֶל־ק֥וֹל הַנַּ֖עַר בַּאֲשֶׁ֥ר
הוּא־שָֽׁם׃

God heard the cry of the boy, and a messenger of God called to Hagar from heaven and said to her, "What troubles you, Hagar? Fear not, for God has heeded the cry of the boy where he is, b'asher hu sham.

After this, Hagar is told to pick up her son and her eyes are opened to a well from which she gives him water to drink. We are told that Yishmael grows up to become a hunter and his mother finds him a wife from Egypt.

In this short narrative the phrase "b'asher hu sham" jumps out to me: the boy's plight is answered "where he is." What does this mean? Why is it important?

One classic answer, provided by Rashi, is that Yishmael is saved, is forgiven, despite the fact that his later descendents will murder Israelites. Yishmael is not judged based on his future, but "according to his present deeds." B'Asher hu sham does more than specify Yishmeal's location, but speaks to his ethical character - he is forgiven as the flawed fallible person he is, as someone who is worth saving now, even though he will sin in the future

The same midrash that Rashi is quoting here starts however, by focusing on the figure of Hagar and her tears over her son's demise. Quoting from Tehillim 39:13 the Midrash states:

שִׁמְעָה תְפִלָּתִי ה' וְשַׁוְעָתִי הַאֲזִינָה וגו', אֶל דִּמְעָתָהּ שֶׁל הָגָר לֹא הֶחֱרַשְׁתָּ אֶל דִּמְעָתִי אַתָּה מַחֲרִישׁ. וְאִם תֹּאמַר עַל יְדֵי שֶׁהָיְתָה גִּיּוֹרֶת הָיְתָה חֲבִיבָה, אַף אָנֹכִי (תהלים לט, יג: (כִּי גֵר אָנֹכִי עִמָּךְ תּוֹשָׁב כְּכָל אֲבוֹתָי

"Hear my prayer, O LORD;/give ear to my cry; etc." To the tears of the Hagar [whose name literally means the stranger] you did not turn a deaf ear, yet to my tears you turn a deaf ear. And if you were to say because she was a foreigner she was beloved, so too me, [and then quoting the end of the verse in Tehillim 39:13] "do not disregard my tears;/for like all my forebears/I am an alien, resident with You."

Hagar's tears are remarkably effective. Although some commentators interpret the text telling us that God specifically "heard the cry of the boy" as meaning that it was Yishmael himself who compelled God's attention, this Midrash explains that it is Hagar, as the stranger, the other, whose cries are efficacious. Hagar is vulnerable, alone, and powerless and yet she cries and prays for another. And for our tears to be effective, we need to see that we too are often, in some way, the stranger.

Indeed, this kind of powerful otherness is one reason the African American community has found in Hagar an inspiring figure for their plight. The theological tradition known as womanism, which explores Christian theology from the perspectives of black women, has particularly been drawn to the character of Hagar. As womanist scholar Delores Williams has written:

> Hagar has 'spoken' to generation after generation of black women because her story has been validated as true by suffering black people. She and Yishmael together, as family, model many black American families in which a lone woman/mother struggles to hold the family together in spite of the poverty to which ruling class economics consign it. Hagar, like many black women, goes into the wide world to make a living for herself and her child, with only God by her side.

Hagar's affecting cries save her fallible, imperfect, human son. The contrast with the story of the Akedah could not be starker. Two aspects of the Akedah are wholly different than in the Hagar and Yishmael story: first Yitzchak is imagined to be perfect and blameless; second a mother figure is entirely and noticeably absent.

Yitzchak's perfection is described in the Midrash as connected to the verse in Tehillim - "יוֹדֵעַ ה' יְמֵי תְמִימִם" - The LORD is concerned for the needs of the blameless." Who is the blameless, the midrash asks? "Ze Yitzchak," "this is Yitzchak." Yitzchak's blamelessness, his perfection is why he can be a korban, a sacrifice, and is why he cannot go down to Egypt later in a time of famine. Yitzchak's salvation at the end of the Akedah is not "b'asher hu sham" - it is not despite his innate sinfulness, but rather because he is perfect.

Yitzchak also lacks a mother, or for that matter a father, crying over him in the Akedah story. From the time of the rabbis until today people have wondered over the lack of Sarah's voice in the Akedah, but it is clear that no one else's tears helped to rescue Yitzchak. He had to be perfect since no one was coming to pray for him.

A contemporary feminist midrash in the collection Dirshuni draws out this contrast. The author, Naama Shaked, imagines what various biblical women might have said to save Yitzchak. Shaked puts the words of the intervening angel from the Akedah story into Sara's mouth - "אל תשלח ידך אל הנער!" "Do not raise your hand against the boy." Sara herself lacks the words and so another character's speech has to be given (back) to her. But no such creative reimagining is required for Hagar who already in the biblical text has powerful words spoken in order to save a son. Shaked's midrash continues with Hagar's words applied to the Akedah:

> Hagar came and said: "אל אראה במות הילד!" "I will not see the child die"! (Genesis 21:16) Sovereign of the world, do as you have done to me, as you say "שמע אלהים אל קול הנער" "God hears the voice of the boy" (ibid., 21:17) and as you said "קומי שאי את הנער והחזיקי את ידך בו" "Arise, lift up the boy and take his hand in yours" (ibid., 21: 18); And what is written after?- "And God opened her eyes" (ibid., 21, 19). Even now, open his, [open Yitzchak's] eyes!

Hagar cries for her child: her tears, her eyes, her cries are able to save an imperfect Yishmael. At the Akedah no one cried, no one prayed, for Yitzchak, the perfect one.

We are not Yitzchak. We are not perfect. We need effective cries, effective prayer. Which means we, like Yishmael, need the prayer of Hagar, who is both a mother and a stranger. Yishmael can be redeemed, can be forgiven, because he is ensconced in a relationship of care, because another cares enough to cry out for him, because of his flaws, because of his vulnerability. Returning to Delores Williams, she notices that in the story of Hagar and Yishmael in the wilderness God commands Hagar to go to

Yishmael, to pick him up and heal him, after promising that he will be saved. Williams writes "God gives [Hagar] a command that, if obeyed, will end the separation between mother and child. Tender loving care is in order. So God bids her to "'Go pick the boy up and hold him safe, for I shall make him into a great nation.' [...]." Hagar and Yishmael 's cries are heard, God saves the boy, because he will be cared for by his mother, who will close the distance between them and embrace him. The two of them together, despite or because of their flaws, are saved by care for the other, b'asher hu sham, as they are now.

In the haftarah for the first day of Rosh Hashana we also heard about the effectiveness of praying for others. Hanna is the model for prayer in Judaism. Her pleas to God for a child, for a baby not yet conceived, for an other for her to care for, to love and worry about, to pray for, were so strong that they become paradigmatic of what it means to pray. Dr. Sarah Zager has written that "experiences of infertility" like Hanna's, "often require substantial 'carework,' but that this 'care work' is for another that remains abstract," akin to how the rabbis see "the future redemption of the Jewish People"as being built on "embodied care" —physical, ritual actions even though "the reality itself remains only imagined and abstract." Hanna prays for another who can not yet be seen, can not yet be imagined - an unknown redemptive future that becomes the model for all prayer.

And Hanna too is prayed for by another: Eli, usually cast negatively in this story, stops long enough to notice, to care for this bereft woman. And when he understands exactly who she is and what she's about, he blesses and prays for her too. Eli eventually comes to a tragic end, and Hanna doesn't reappear in the story after bringing her prayed-for son to the Mishkan. But the object of their prayer, the prophet Shmuel, not only goes on to fulfill their prayers but is part of the redemption of Israel.

Rosh Hashannah and Yom Kippur Musaf begin with one of my favorite liturgical moments in the whole year - the Hineni prayer that just the Shaliach Tzibur recites. This too is prayer about the power of praying for others:

> "I have come to stand and to plead before You on behalf of Your people, Yisrael, who have appointed me their messenger; even though I am not worthy or qualified for the task. [...] Do not hold them responsible for my sins, nor condemn them for my iniquities, as I am a sinner and a transgressor. Let them not be disgraced through my transgressions; may they not be ashamed of me, nor may I be ashamed of them."

What a moment - the designated emissary of the community who we have entrusted to communicate with God, saying "I am fallible, I have sinned, I am only human" and pleading for forgiveness because he is praying on behalf of others. He may not be worthy, but still his heartfelt prayers for others can be heard and received, allowing the community's prayers to be heard as well. He needs to be heard by God b'asher hu sham, where he is, and so do we.

When we pray for ourselves, we cannot know if our prayers will be heard. We could try and be like Yitzchak and strive for perfection, but let's face it, we inevitably fail. We need to be heard and be forgiven b'asher hu sham. But like with Hagar, like with Hanna, and like with the shaliach tzibur, our prayers just might be answered, our tears turned to joy, when we pray for others. When we sit with Hagar for a moment and realize she is the stranger, ha'ger, whose prayers for her child are answered, and we too are strangers who need others to pray for, and who need people to pray for us.

And so too, we pray in community. It's in the community where we pray together, and we pray for one another, that we become forceful, that our words become effective, that our prayers are answered, that we achieve teshuva.

So let's consider what we are praying for, who we are praying with, who we are praying for and who is praying for us. It's in the neighbor, familiar or new, who's sitting next to you that redemption can be found, redemption as we are now, b'asher hu sham.

Through the gate of the Irat Chamaïm, towards the Simha

Myriam Goldwasser
Paris, August 8, 2023

The source of these teachings must remain a secret, for, being a woman, I have, as I have been told many times, neither the right to hear them nor the right to understand them. Yet they have fed me where my greatest thirst was. This thirst has allowed me to be patient. It also enabled me to marvel at the depth of this Rav's Emounah, his sincerity and generosity in conveying to us, beyond words, the firmness of the link to the Divine in all circumstances.

It enables me today to get through a serious illness without terror, to hold together the will to heal and use this nissaion to strengthen my Bitahon, and that of bearing witness to the message of one who, for me, is a hidden Tsaddik, a message that can bring us closer to our innermost truth.

Twice, the secretary called to tell me that this was a course for men. Twice the number was changed. The course was, and still is, for men only, and a certain ultra-Orthodox tradition expresses clearly elsewhere that the place of men is in the study, that of women in the home, that their roles are complementary and not substitutable. This is perhaps the first time in Paris that a woman has ventured into a men-only class for three years, since the technical revolution led the ultra-Orthodox rabbinate, in the midst of the Covid 19 crisis, to allow hybrid group classes, on site at the Kollel and at a distance, by phone. In any case, this is the first time this experience has been written up and published.

Beyond the ordinary human nature that led me to want even more what was forbidden to me, there was, for me, a vital stake in this: after the Shoah, which had destroyed my parents' Emounah in the face of the horror of the camps, to learn how to believe in God beyond the disaster, how to rebuild myself and rediscover within myself this difficult path towards light, hope and joy.

To do this, I had to be humble: in the class, I couldn't say hello, goodbye or thank you, I had to be perfectly invisible, I had to blend into the telephone wire.

This book took the form of a long journey through the weekly parachot, during three complete circles of the Houmash, in 2021, 2022 and 2023. Woven patiently over the phone line, in the silence of my home, it is intended only as an introduction to ultra-Orthodox Jewish thought, highlighting the link between our past and our present, between the reading of traditional texts and our daily life and thought. It shows the major importance of an original and well-structured ultra-Orthodox teaching, for all those interested in the Jewish faith, who want to acquire a profound knowledge of it. I'm not going to discuss the machism I experiment, because that's not the point. It's true that I disobey a prohibition to give birth to this book. What counts, in my opinion, is the quality of this living, up-to-date teaching, for nourishing our intelligence and bringing us closer to the Presence. Perhaps one day, in the dedication, I'll be able to thank the person who allowed me to write it, and who unknowingly enlightened my life when I couldn't say hello nor goodbye.

Here's an excerpt, which I can take no credit for other than having understood and transcribed. It highlights the importance of the Irat Chamaïm in approaching the Torah, especially for the Tichri Iomim Tovim but also, through this door, the extraordinary proximity of the Shekhinah in the Simha.

Course of 09/14/2022 (excerpts)

"He who hears the voice of gladness and joy, thanks Hashem. He who listens to Divreï Torah, he will see this. He who studies can understand, integrate that.

It's said that two Rahamim, two sages, in the minian are enough to change dimension. The greatness of Torah is hidden in this world, but he who listens will see its greatness. He will rise in both worlds, because he has studied it. You can study far away, but you have to integrate what you heard, things have to be translated in your own perception of the world and of things, and like that, little by little, the Torah changes me, that's what it means to listen. I'm not only here to understand, but also to elevate myself. It comes from a higher level than me, and it can elevate me. These are not concepts, nor are they ordinary ideas. The Beit a Knesset is not my ordinary home either. I have to become aware of where I am.

Hashem says: Blessed is he who listens to me. Blessed is he.

Why do I study? Because I want to be close to Hashem. So I do it out of love, out of love for Hashem.

It's said that you shouldn't stand at the door of the house of study, that you should enter. One door after another. The midrash says my doors, not my door, and often in a synagogue there are two doors, and Hashem counts your steps. The Loubavitch Hasidim often count an hour before praying, they prepare, reading the psalms, because the level of Tefila requires preparation.

If the Shul is far away, you can also prepare during your walking. The two gates in the building of the Shul represent this time of preparation.

Hashem says, he who enters, will keep my mezuzot. In a Beit a Knesset, mezuzot are not obligatory. The person who comes in is compared to a mezuzah, and is told: "You too, don't move from my door, try to come as much as possible into the Beit a Knesset, as into a place from which you don't want to move. Except for studying elsewhere. If you really do so, you'll find yourself face to face with the Shekhinah, the divine presence.

For Hashem says: he who has found me, has found life.

And if you haven't found my presence, you haven't really listened.

He who truly listens comes face to face with the Shekhinah and receives an elevation.

The Beit a Knesset is the place where to experience this, and so is the Beit a Midrash.

You have to be ready to perceive it, to be aware that there's something there that I can't see. You need Irat Chamaïm, sacred fear, to know that Hashem resides there.

That's why we don't do little talk in the Shul. We want to hear, to perceive, because I want this closeness to Hashem. The midrash clearly promises us this elevation on condition that we know how to detach ourselves from the outside world. Hashem stands where there's an assembly. There, we can find life, receive Hashem's benevolence, his Brahot, his blessings.

I necessarily receive these Brahot by listening to something greater than myself, if I really wants it.

You can also miss out on all this, depending on how you enter the Beit a Knesset.

You have to listen beyond your understanding to hear the voice of joy. It's a voice that will move you deeply. The voice of a true Simha. And even if your level is low, you can rejoice with Her, together. You'll see and experience that joy. (There's a precise study on this subject in the Oral Torah) You have to know that you must first detach yourself from any disturbance and listen only to that voice, and you'll move forward."

This course gives us a clear direction, reminding us that Torah is really accessible, here and now, and that we can, all, with the right preparation and concentration, enter into communication with the Divine through Joy. The appointments of the Iomim Tovim, if they are to fill us with Irat Chamaïm, are essentially promises of connection, of repeated and strengthened contact with the Divine who gives us life and carries us beyond ourselves on the side of truth, of reality. They are the Light that will enable us, all year round, to live in the proximity of the shadow without loosing our sense of self. They are the Joy, the Simha through which we can glimpse into the Beauty of the created world and, in unity with this world, give thanks.

Israel rejoices and will rejoice on the breast of her Creator (Psalm 149), or in her body. Or in her womb of life. In harmony with the created world, where every herb, stone and tree raises its voice to praise Hashem with its own tone. Col a Nechama Tehallel Ia Allelouia (Psalm 150) Every living soul Praises You in the Hallel, rises and will rise.

Par la porte de l'Irat Chamaïm, vers la Simha

Myriam Goldwasser
Paris, August 8, 2023.

La source de ces enseignements doit rester secrète, car, étant une femme, je n'ai, on me l'a répété plusieurs fois, ni le droit de les entendre ni celui de les comprendre. Ils m'ont pourtant nourrie là où était ma plus grande soif. Cette soif-là a permis ma patience. Elle m'a permis aussi de m'émerveiller devant la profondeur de la Emounah de ce Rav, sa sincérité, et sa générosité, pour nous transmettre, au-delà des mots, la fermeté du lien au Divin en toutes circonstances.

Elle me permet aujourd'hui de traverser une maladie grave sans terreur, de tenir ensemble la volonté de vivre, de guérir, et d'utiliser cette épreuve pour renforcer mon Bitahon, et celle de témoigner du message de celui qui, pour moi, est un Tsaddik caché, message qui peut nous rapprocher de notre intime vérité.

Deux fois, la secrétaire m'a appelée pour me dire que c'était un cours pour les hommes. Deux fois, le numéro d'appel a été modifié. Le cours était, est toujours, réservé aux hommes, et une certaine tradition ultra-orthodoxe exprime clairement ailleurs que la place des hommes est à l'étude, celle des femmes à la maison, que leurs rôles sont complémentaires et non substituables. C'est donc peut-être la première fois qu'à Paris, une femme s'aventure, pendant trois ans, à suivre un cours réservé aux hommes, depuis que la révolution technique a conduit, en pleine crise de Covid 19, le rabbinat ultra-orthodoxe à permettre lui aussi des cours collectifs hybrides, sur place au Kollel, et à distance, au téléphone. En tout cas, c'est la première fois que cette expérience est écrite, que ce témoignage débouche sur une publication.

Au-delà de la nature humaine ordinaire qui me conduisait à vouloir encore plus ce qui m'était interdit, il y a eu, pour moi, en cela, un enjeu vital : après la Shoah, qui avait détruit la Emounah de mes parents devant l'horreur des camps, apprendre comment croire au-delà du désastre, comment me reconstruire et retrouver en moi ce chemin difficile vers la lumière, l'espoir, et la joie.

J'ai dû pour cela faire preuve d'humilité, je ne pouvais dire ni bonjour ni au revoir ni merci, il fallait que mon invisibilité soit parfaite, que je me fonde dans le fil du téléphone.

Ce livre a pris la forme d'un long voyage dans les parachot hebdomadaires, nourri de trois cercles complets dans le Houmash, en 2021, 2022 et 2023. Tissé de patience au fil du téléphone, dans le silence complice de ma maison, il se veut seulement une initiation à la pensée juive ultra-orthodoxe, qui met en relief le lien entre notre passé et notre présent, entre la lecture des textes traditionnels et notre vie et notre pensée quotidiennes. Il montre l'actualité brûlante d'un enseignement ultra-orthodoxe érudit, original et bien structuré, pour tous ceux et toutes celles qui s'intéressent à la foi juive, et veulent en acquérir une connaissance profonde. Je fais ici abstraction du machisme que j'ai subi, parce que ce n'est pas l'important. Certes, j'ai désobéi à un interdit pour que naisse ce livre. Ce qui compte, à mon avis, c'est la qualité de cet enseignement actuel et vivant, pour nourrir notre intelligence et nous rapprocher de la Présence. Un jour, peut-être, je pourrai, dans la dédicace, remercier celui qui m'a permis de l'écrire et qui a éclairé ma vie sans le savoir, quand je ne pouvais dire ni bonjour ni au-revoir.

En voici un extrait, que je n'ai d'autre mérite qu'avoir compris et retranscrit. Il met en évidence l'importance de l'Irat Chamaïm dans l'abord de la Torah mais aussi , par cette porte, l'extraordinaire proximité de la Shekhinah dans la Simha.

Cours du 14/09/2022 (extraits)

> « Celui qui entend la voix de l'allégresse et de la joie, remercie Hachem. Celui qui écoute Divreï Torah, il verra cela. Celui qui étudie peut comprendre, s'imprégner.
>
> On dit qu'avec deux Rahamim, deux sages, dans le minian, çà suffit pour changer de dimension. La grandeur de la Torah est cachée dans ce monde, mais celui qui écoute verra sa grandeur. Il s'élèvera dans les deux mondes, parce qu'il s'est penché sur elle. On peut étudier lointain mais il faut intégrer ce qu'on entend, les choses doivent être replacées dans notre propre perception du monde et des choses, et comme cela, petit à petit, la Torah me modifie, c'est çà que signifie entendre. Je ne suis pas seulement là pour comprendre mais aussi pour m'élever. Ca vient d'un niveau plus élevé que moi et çà peut m'élever moi. Ce ne sont pas des concepts, ni des idées habituelles. Le Beit a Knesset, la synagogue, n'est pas non plus ma demeure ordinaire. Je dois y prendre conscience de où je suis. Hachem dit : Heureux celui qui m'écoute.
>
> Pourquoi j'étudie ? Parce que je veux une proximité avec Hachem. Je le fais donc par amour, par amour pour Hachem.

On dit qu'il ne faut pas rester à la porte pour étudier, qu'il faut entrer. Une porte après l'autre, le midrash dit mes portes, pas ma porte, et souvent dans une synagogue il y a deux portes, et Hachem compte tes pas. Les Hassidim comptent une heure avant de prier, ils se préparent, en lisant les psaumes, parce que le niveau de Tefila demande une préparation. Si la Shoule est loin, en marchant on peut se préparer aussi. Les deux portes représentent ce temps où l'on doit se préparer. Hachem dit, celui qui entre, garde mes mezouzot. Dans un Beit a Knesset, les mezouzot ne sont pas obligatoires. La personne qui vient est comparée à une mezouzah, on lui dit : toi aussi, ne bouge pas de ma porte, cherche à venir le plus possible dans le Beit a Knesset, comme dans un endroit d'où tu ne veux pas bouger. Sauf pour aller étudier. Si tu le fais vraiment, tu te trouveras en face de la Shekhinah, de la présence divine.

Car Hachem dit : celui qui m'a trouvé, a trouvé la vie.
Et celui qui n'a pas trouvé ma présence, c'est qu'il n'a pas vraiment écouté.
Celui qui écoute vraiment se retrouve face à la Shekhinah et s'imprègne d'une élévation.
Le Beit a Knesset est l'endroit où l'on doit sentir cela, le Beit a Midrash aussi.
Il faut être prêt pour le percevoir, être conscient qu'il y a quelque chose que je ne vois pas qui est là. Il faut la Irat Chamaïm, la crainte sacrée, pour savoir que Hachem réside là.
C'est pour çà qu'on ne discute pas. On veut entendre, percevoir, parce que je veux cette proximité avec Hachem. J'entre sans mon portable… Le midrash nous promet clairement cette élévation à condition que nous sachions nous détacher du monde extérieur. Hachem se tient là où il y a une assemblée. On peut y trouver la vie, y recevoir la bienveillance de Hachem, ses Brahot, ses bénédictions.

Je reçois nécessairement ces Brahot en me mettant à l'écoute de quelque chose qui est plus grand que moi, à condition de le vouloir.

On peut aussi rater tout çà, tout dépend de la manière dont on entre au Beit a Knesset.

Il faut écouter au-delà de sa compréhension pour entendre la voix de la joie. On entend cette voix qui est touchante. La voix d'une vraie Simha. Et même si tu n'es pas au niveau tu pourras te réjouir avec elle, ensemble. Tu verras et éprouveras cette joie. (Il y a une étude sur cela dans la Torah orale) Il faut savoir que tu dois te détacher d'abord de tout dérangement et écouter seulement cette voix, et tu avanceras. »

Ce cours nous donne une direction claire, il nous rappelle que la Torah est accessible réellement, ici et maintenant, et que nous pouvons, tous et toutes, par une préparation et une concentration adéquates, entrer en communication avec le Divin par la Joie. Les rendez-vous des Iomim Tovim , s'ils doivent nous remplir de Irat Chamaïm, sont essentiellement des promesses de lien, de contact répété et affermi avec le Divin qui nous donne vie et nous porte au-delà de nous-même du côté de la vérité, de la réalité. Ils sont la Lumière qui nous permettra, toute l'année, de côtoyer l'ombre sans nous y confondre. Ils sont la Joie, la Simha par laquelle nous pouvons apercevoir la Beauté du monde créé et, avec elle, remercier.

Israël se réjouit et se réjouira au sein de son Créateur.(Psaume 149) Ou dans son ventre. Ou dans sa matrice de vie. Au sein du monde créé où chaque herbe, chaque pierre, chaque arbre, fait entendre sa voix pour louer Hachem à sa manière. Col a Nechama Tehallel Ia Allelouia .(Psaume 150) Chaque âme vivante Te Loue dans le Hallel, s'élève et s'élèvera.

Trauma and Recovery:
Abraham's Journey to the Akeidah[1]

Naomi Graetz

This article originally appeared in the Central Conference of American Rabbis Spring 2012 Quarterly Journal. Reprinted with permission of the author.

In the concluding paragraph of an article on the *Akeidah*, the late Tikva Frymer Kensky wrote that "in its stark horror and ambiguous statements, the story of the *Akedah* remains the central text in the formation of our spiritual consciousness."[2] In Genesis 22:1 it begins, "After these things, God tested (*nisah*) Abraham," in which God asks Abraham to sacrifice his son. As Wendy Zierler puts it, "Abraham offers no emotional or ethical response to the command. He simply sets out with his son to do God's bidding."[3] The *Akeidah* (Gen. 22:1–19), the binding of Isaac, is considered to be *the* ultimate spiritual moment, when a man expresses willingness to sacrifice his beloved son to demonstrate fealty to his Lord. This central text has continued to horrify generations, and in Sören Kierkegaard's words, arouses "fear and trembling."[4]

The Hebrew for a burnt offering that goes up to God is *olah and* is used to describe Abraham's offering of his son. The Sages understand the test (from the word *nisah*) to mean a trial, one of many trials — physical and psychological incidents that retarded Abraham's adjustment in Canaan and endangered his marital status.[5] According to the midrash, fiery associations are among the many obstacles Abraham had in his journey before he got to the point of bringing his son Isaac as an *olah*. Another obstacle was the famine in the land, which caused Abraham to go down to Egypt.

The *King James Bible*, however, translates the word, *nisah,* as "tempt," not as "test"! To tempt is to solicit to sin, to entice, to entrap, with the purpose of bringing about the fall of a person. The *KJV* may have translated it in this way because the translators were influenced by Rashi's reading of the Talmud. If that is so, then who is the subject of the temptation?

> "SOME TIME AFTERWARDS" Some of our Rabbis say (BT Sanhedrin 89) that this line refers to after the incident with Satan who accused [God] saying "From all of the festive meals that Abraham made, he did not offer You a single bull or ram." God responded, "Everything Abraham did was for his son. Yet, if I were to tell Abraham to sacrifice him before me, he would not delay." (Rashi, 22:1)

Is it God being tempted to play with Abraham, as he did with Job?[6] Or is God testing Abraham to see if he gives into the temptation of filicide that was widespread in his time?

One might ask where God was during these trials or temptations. Why was there lack of moral guidance to Abraham? From a theological perspective, what is worse, the problem of an abusive God/father who demands sacrifices of his son/people or a God who tempts people to sin?

Looking at Abraham from a relationship perspective and in particular with his troubling relationship with God, I can understand the transition in his character from one who fights back to protect his family and the other who abandons his family to fate. There is no contradiction if we view Abraham as a person who has experienced trauma and abuse as a son, a brother, a husband, and a believer. If we regard him as a multiple victim of PTSD (post-traumatic stress disorder), then Abraham behaves consistently when he heeds God's call to sacrifice Isaac. To see how this works, we must look at the back story of Abraham's life, which is to be found in Rabbinic midrash and commentary. It is possible to argue that the midrashim we will be looking at are supplying us with the original "censored" text, especially the one having to do with Abraham's near death by Nimrod in the furnace.[7] We will start with two midrashim that explain Haran's death.

The first one depicts Terah as a manufacturer of idols. Abraham destroyed these idols. His father was furious and seized him and delivered him to Nimrod. Nimrod throws him into the fiery furnace saying, "Behold, I will cast you into it, and let your God whom you adore come and save you from it."

> Now Haran was standing there undecided. If Abram is victorious, [thought he], I will say that I am of Abram's belief, while if Nimrod is victorious, I will say that I am on Nimrod's side. When Abram descended into the fiery furnace and was saved, he [Nimrod] asked him, "Of whose belief are you?" "Of Abram's," he replied. Thereupon he seized and cast him into the fire; his inwards were scorched, and he died in his father's presence. Hence it is written, AND HARAN DIED IN THE PRESENCE OF [AL P'NEI] HIS FATHER TERAH.[8]

The Rabbis translated al p'nei as "because of"; that is, he died because his father manufactured idols!

According to Aviva Zornberg in her book The Murmuring Deep, "Nachmanides treats the fiery furnace midrash as not only historically true but essential for the meaning of Abraham's narrative." There is no good reason why this narrative is omitted from the biblical text, but as Zornberg points out, "the repressed persecution story leaves us with a significant gap."[9] She states the case even more strongly:

> In this stark retelling of the midrash, the essential fact is that Abraham's brother was killed by his father, who had originally intended Abraham's own death. By handing him over for execution, Terah is, virtually, killing him. And when

he is saved, his brother's actual death is directly attributable to Terah . . . This memory of horror is not recorded in the written biblical text.[10]

The other midrash is less well known and speaks of attempted fratricide:

And Haran died "*al p'nei*" his father Terah. Until this time no son had died before the father. And this one, why did he die? Because of what happened in Ur Casdim. When Abram was shattering Terah's idols; and they were jealous of him and threw him into the fiery furnace. And Haran stood by, adding fuel to the fire and was enthusiastic about the flames. Therefore, it is said that Haran died before his father Terah. In Ur Casdim. The name of the place is like the fire (*urim*), relying on a verse from Isaiah 24:15, "honor the Lord with lights."[11]

In this source Haran is among those jealous of Abraham and fanatically wishes to participate in his murder. Haran is the one, in this text, who is in charge of stoking the fire in the furnace, and he is in the process of feeding the fire when the flames shoot out and consume him. In this Midrash both the brother and father are out to kill Abraham. Haran is gleeful while making the fire as hot as possible so that killing Abraham will "make his day." Thus, according to these two midrashim, Abraham has experienced abuse at the hand of Nimrod the king, his father, his brother, and indirectly by God. Besides using the tools of Rabbinic midrash and later looking at some modern poetry to comprehend Abraham's action, I find Judith Herman's book *Trauma and Recovery* very useful for her description of PTSD:[12]

> Traumatic events are extraordinary, not because they occur rarely, but rather because they overwhelm the ordinary human adaptations to life. Unlike commonplace misfortunes, traumatic events generally involve threats to

life or bodily integrity, or a close personal encounter with violence and death.[13]

This of course is what, according to the midrash, Abraham has certainly experienced. Herman writes that "the person may feel as if the event is not happening to [him]...a bad dream from which [he] will shortly awaken."[14] Herman points out that the victim who suffers from PTSD may feel a state of detached calm, in which terror, rage, and pain dissolve . . . Perceptions may be numbed or distorted . . . Time sense may be altered, often with a sense of slow motion.[15]

These may have been Abraham's feelings as he went up the mountain, slowly but inexorably.

When we return to Genesis 11:26–32, we find lacunae that leave much to the imagination. The text does not say why they left, nor does it say why they stayed in Charan. Was Terah alive when Abraham and Lot left? What did Abraham feel about leaving? Would he have liked to stay and comfort his father? Did his love for God get in the way of making amends with his father?

Clearly there is a need for even more "back story," which the commentators and the midrash continue to provide. According to Ibn Ezra on Genesis 12:1, Abraham's father, Terah, lived for another sixty-five years in Haran and in taking his grandson Lot away from him, he severed the family relationship and deprived Terah of his grandson Lot. When the family leaves Egypt, after strife with Lot, Abraham proposes that his nephew's herdsmen separate from his. Abraham already separated Lot from his grandfather and country and now he does so from himself.

Why is Abraham so much a master at separation from his close family? Is this a fatal flaw in him? According to Judith

Herman, "The core experiences of psychological trauma are disempowerment and disconnection from others."[16] If this is so, can it account for Abraham's ease in letting Lot go, then Sarah (with the real possibility of losing her), and then Hagar and Ishmael and finally Isaac? It would seem that the Sages picked up on this as well. For in a famous midrash the Rabbis try to change the order of the text to show that Terah died in Charan.[17] Why do they do this? To show that Terah was wicked, and like all wicked, are called dead even during their lifetime. Why do they do this? They do this so as not to detract from Abraham's greatness.

Yet in this same midrash we read that Abraham was afraid that people would say, "He left his father in his old age and departed." Therefore, God reassured him by saying: "I exempt thee (*l'cha*) from the duty of honoring thy parents, though I exempt no one else from this duty." The Rabbis deduced this from the emphasis GET THEE (*LECH L'CHA*), where *lech* (go) alone would have sufficed. And this is why God recorded Terah's death before Abraham departed. So one part of the midrash implies that Terah is the old father that Abraham dishonorably leaves behind, and the other says that Terah is an evil person whom Abraham had the *right* to leave behind.

What are we to make of this contradiction? I find it strange that the Rabbis would prefer to reverse the order of the biblical text rather than acknowledge that Abraham had the right to detach himself from a possibly abusive father. In reading Kierkegaard, I am struck by how the second half of the midrash is a perfect example of the "teleological suspension of the ethical." And this first act of "suspension of the ethical" later permits him to do other unethical acts.[18] Could it be that the Rabbis sensed something murky in Abraham's past when they referred to him as a Job-like figure and vice versa and that God's test of Abraham is similar to Job's because of Satan's intervention?[19]

71

What are we to make of a God who submits to a challenge of Satan and plays with people like sport to the flies? Who unfairly puts his people to a test, puts temptation in their way, to see how great is their faith, their love for Him?

It is difficult to accept Kierkegaard's conclusion that God tempted Abraham to prove his faith by rejecting morality.[20] This kind of faith is seen by many as "religious" only in an extreme or fanatical way, and as such a kind of idolatry, or perversion of religion, which always factors in a moral dimension. Besides what does God gain by having an exemplar of faith act immorally? Why tempt him to do so? This is the *sine qua non* question that has plagued generations of readers, both religious and secular, when they confront the text of the *Akeidah*.

In previous work I have discussed the effects of a God who abuses his people.[21] Some of these images include executioner, mass murderer, and divine deceiver. These images are problematic because God acts unethically or immorally, uses excessive force, and sometimes doesn't offer an opportunity for repentance.[22] Most of us would prefer not to contemplate a God who is too dangerous to approach and too incomprehensible to make sense of, a God who might simply demand extreme and devastating behavior. We avoid all thought of the paradox that the very foundation of the world might also contribute to its devastation.[23]

Another troubling image of God that I will point to briefly, since I have written so much about this elsewhere, is that of God the husband/lover of Israel, who has total power over his female people. In one midrash we see Abraham depicted as a woman, a daughter whose father owns the house she lives in and is aroused by her beauty and wants to show it off to the world.

NOW THE LORD SAID UNTO ABRAM: Go Forth from your Land etc. (12:1). R. Isaac commenced his discourse with, 'Listen daughter, and look and incline your ear; and forget your people, and your father's house (Ps. 45:11).' R. Isaac said: This is a *mashal*, about someone who traveled from place to place and saw a *birah* (building, castle, capital city) burning. He wondered: Is it possible that this *birah* doesn't have a leader? The owner/master of the *birah* looked out and said, "I am the master of the birah." Similarly, since our father Abraham was constantly wondering, "Is it conceivable that the world is without a leader/guide/master/ruler?" God looked out and said to him, "I am the *ba'al*, the owner of the world, the Sovereign of the Universe." So let the king be aroused by your beauty, since he is your lord (Ps. 45:12): Let the king be aroused by your beauty and show it off to the world. Since he is your lord, bow to him (Ps. 45:12): hence, THE LORD SAID UNTO ABRAHAM: Go forth etc.[24]

Abraham is again depicted as a woman, this time as the unformed little sister, in another midrash on the same verse.[25] Here she offers herself up to be sacrificed in an act of *kiddush HaShem* or martyrdom. The idea that God is Abraham's lover appears also in Maimonides in the *Mishneh Torah*. Here it is Abraham who is obsessed with God and has what can only be described as lovesickness.

Halacha 2: [Love] is an attribute of Abraham our father, who was called "his beloved" because he worshiped him out of love. And it is a quality that was commanded by Moses in that we are to "worship our God" . . .

Halacha 3: What characterizes proper love? That a person should love God with a great excessive, very strong love, until one's soul is bound up in love of God and is obsessed by this love as if he is lovesick; and his mind is not freed from the love of that woman; and he is always obsessed by her, whether it is in his resting or rising, or whether he is

73

eating or drinking. Moreover, the love of God in the heart of those who love Him is obsessive, like the commandment to love with all your heart and soul (Deut. 6:5). This is alluded to by Solomon who stated through the Mashal, "for I am sick with love" and in fact all of the Song of Songs is a mashal/parable about this issue.[26]

Rabbinic literature is sensitive to these images of God the lover and the obsession with the beloved, but do not necessarily see them as troubling, full of potential menace, and contributing to abuse. Love sickness is pathological by nature — it affects decision making, it distracts one from what is moral. It further dislocates one who is already fragile.[27] Furthermore, love should not harm.[28]

When Abraham is depicted as a dependent woman, he is, like Herman's traumatized patient, primed for God:[29] "The greater the patient's emotional conviction of helplessness and abandonment, the more desperately she feels the need for an omnipotent rescuer."[30] The fact that he loves God and God loves him makes it seem natural to follow God to wherever and whatever he demands.

Despite the threats hanging over him, the Rabbis are at great pains to make it look as if Abraham is an active willing participant in what God demanded of him. A midrash says that God was with him when he willingly offered (*nadavta*) . . . to enter the fiery furnace and would have emigrated sooner to the land if he had been permitted to do so earlier.[31]

What is the nature of the God Abraham is expected to follow? The Rabbis write that this God places the righteous in doubt and suspense, and then He reveals to them the meaning of the matter. That is why it is written, "TO THE LAND THAT I WILL SHOW THEE." The Rabbis view this putting of the "righteous in doubt and suspense" as a sign of God's love.

> R. Levi said: "Get thee" is written twice, and we do not know which was more precious [in the eyes of God], whether the first or the second . . . And why did He not reveal it to him [without delay]? In order to make him even more beloved in his eyes and reward him for every word spoken, for R. Huna said in R. Eliezer's name: *The Holy One, blessed be He, first places the righteous in doubt and suspense,* and then He reveals to them the meaning of the matter. Thus, it is written, TO THE LAND THAT I WILL SHOW THEE; Upon one of the mountains which I will tell thee of; And make unto it the proclamation that I bid thee (Jonah III, 2); Arise, go forth into the plain, and I will there speak with thee (Ezek. III, 22).[32]

In addition, the Rabbis are making an equation between *Lech L'cha* and the *Akeidah*. *Lech L'cha* is also a foundational text, because it encourages (perhaps in the case of going up to the Land of Israel, even enshrines) leaving loved ones behind and it encourages detachment. Perhaps if Abraham (and others who wish to leave) would think it out clearly, they might hesitate to follow the lure of *Lech L'cha*. In both cases God does not reveal his intentions to Abraham until the very end.[33]

Zornberg refers to Rashi's explication of the verse "to the land that I will show you." Rashi writes that God "did not reveal which land immediately, in order to make it precious in his eyes." Zorn berg builds on this to show that "the effect of suspended naming is to achieve an intimacy . . . tantalize him and endow him with an experience of mystery." She interprets this as suspense. She de scribes this as follows: "He will travel without solid ground under his feet . . . [he will be] off balance . . . [it will be] a painfully tantalizing process, in which delay only increases the horror of real ization."[34] Whereas she reads this positively, I read this as further abuse. Instead of giving Abraham agency, God keeps him in his power and cruelly tantalizes him until the end. Surely this is not a sign of love.

In a transaction with Abraham in Genesis 15, God appears to Abraham in a *machazeh* (a vision), telling him that he will protect him and provide for him. Following the *b'rit bein habetarim* (the covenant of the pieces of animals), Abraham falls asleep, and a great dread of darkness falls upon him. He has a nightmarish vision of a smoking oven and a flaming torch, which according to Zornberg reminds him of Nimrod's fi re. She writes that forgotten, repressed, absent from the biblical text, is the story of the fiery furnace, in which the child Abraham was thrown, to test his faith in the invisible God . . . Its total absence from the written biblical text suggest that it is an unthinkable, even an unbearable narrative, banished from Abraham's memory.[35]

It is unbearable because Abraham is being treated as a pawn by God. If he were truly a partner, God would share with him what is on his mind, so that Abraham can react appropriately, take into account all options and then make up his own mind. On the surface, this is what God seems to do in Genesis 18:17 when he says: "Am I to hide [lit. cover up, *mechaseh*] from Abraham that thing which I do."

Initially God treats him as a full partner, but since He goes on his way to do what he had planned to do all along, destroy the town and its evil inhabitants (except for Lot and all his family), what is Abraham to make of all this? Why did he not continue to protest? Did he end up being a passive bystander, or was he complicit in the destruction as the Israeli poet Meir Wieseltier (b. 1941) writes in his poem "Abraham":

76

The only thing in the world that Abraham loved was God.
He did not love the gods of other men,
Which were made of wood or clay and of polished vermilion
. . .
He did not appreciate anything in the world, only God.
He never sinned to Him; there was no difference between
them.
Not like Isaac, who loved his coarse-minded son; not like
Jacob Who slaved away for women, who limped from the
blows that God gave him at night,
Who saw angelic ladders only in dreams.
Not so Abraham, who loved God, and whom God loved,
And together they counted the righteous of the city before
they wiped it out.

Wieseltier sees a straight line from Abraham's willingness to
see Sodom wiped out and his willingness to sacrifice Isaac in
the name of love.

I would not go so far; for I see his acquiescence to what
eventually happens as being the way a traumatized soul such
as Abram has reacted to what has happened in his past—and
he has already done the unthinkable by casting out his first-
born son.

Yet one can argue that Abraham shows great initiative in
Genesis 14 when invaders took his nephew Lot from Sodom. I
use Her man's words to view this is as a form of recovery
[which] is based upon the empowerment of the survivor and
the creation of new connections. Recovery can take place only
within the context of relationships; it cannot occur in isolation.
In [his] renewed connections with other people, the survivor
re-creates the psychological faculties that were damaged or
deformed by the traumatic experience.[36]

Thus, when Abram heard that his kinsman had been taken
captive, he went in pursuit as far as Dan and brought back Lot

and his pos sessions. And when the king of Sodom said to Abram, "Give me the persons, and take the possessions for yourself," Abram said to the king of Sodom, "I swear to the Lord, I will not take so much as a thread or a sandal strap of what is yours; you shall not say, 'It is I who made Abram rich.'" So it is here that Abraham takes the moral high ground, something he has never done before.

Unfortunately, this is to prove the exception to what I am claiming is his usual way of acting and Abraham reverts to his previous behavior in Genesis 16 when the story of the interaction between Sarai and Hagar is highlighted. Without any protest, Abram passively heeds Sarai's request to take Hagar so she can have a son through her. When Sarai blames Abram, "The wrong done me is your fault!" (*chamasi alecha*), and makes him feel guilty, Abram again passively gives in to Sarai and says, "Your maid is in your hands. Deal with her as you think right." Why this lack of concern about his potential seed? Is it fear of his wife? Is it because he knows that Sarah was also once taken and traumatized? Is this why he allows her some leeway when she lashes at those around her? It doesn't help that God condones Sarah's abusive behavior through His agent who tells Hagar to submit to this abuse from Sarah. I don't want to exonerate Abraham because of the abuse he has suffered in the past, but it seems that Herman's explanation, about the cycle of abuse passing on, is valid here. Herman writes:

> The protracted involvement with the perpetrator has altered the patient's relational style, so that [he] not only fears repeated victimization but also seems unable to protect [him]self from it, or even appears to invite it. The dynamics of dominance and sub mission are reenacted in all subsequent relationships.[37]

For sure the trauma that afflicted Abraham is passed on to Isaac in the form of passivity in the face of abuse — and this trait will be passed on to the biblical family. Abraham's tears, according to the midrash, blinded Isaac. As he held the knife "tears streamed from his eyes, and these tears, prompted by a father's compassion, dropped into Isaac's eyes."[38] And Isaac will, in turn, turn a blind eye to the cheating and neglect that Rebekah and Jacob inflict on Esau. Jacob, too, will be a passive parent when it comes to not seeing the family dynamics taking place with his own children. The inappropriate parenting that has taken place in Abraham's household is thus passed on to the next generation.

In addition to trauma and abuse, there is also the issue of attachment and lack of attachment. There are many types of attachment. John Bowlby was the first to use the term when he encountered trauma during World War II. He described attachment as a "lasting psychological connectedness between human beings."[39] He believed that the emotional bonds formed by children with their mothers had a continuous impact on their life choices. In this theory it is important that mothers are available to their child's needs and that the child knows that the mother can be depended on to give him a sense of security. Abraham's father is identified in the bible, but his mother is given only a name in the Talmud — Amathlai the daughter of Karnebo:

> R. Hanan b. Raba further stated in the name of Rab: [The name of] the mother of Abraham [was] Amathlai, the daughter of Karnebo [from Kar, "lamb," Nevo ("Mount of) Nebo"]; [the name of] the mother of Haman was Amathlai, the daughter of Orabti [from Oreb, "raven"] and your mnemonic [may be], "unclean [to] unclean, clean [to] clean." [Haman's grandmother was named after an unclean animal (raven, cf. Lev. 11:15; Deut. 14:14); but Abra ham's grandmother bore the name of a clean animal.][40]

I am assuming Amathlai was never present for Abraham in his life. One can only speculate on her absence and her detachment from her three sons, and it is not clear what purpose the Midrash has in even assigning her a name—and more curious the connection to Haman's mother.

Perhaps the Talmudic text hints at an insecure attachment that is caused by stressful life events, such as neglect, death, abuse, and migration. In this situation you keep looking and hoping that someone or something will come about to give you back what you lost.[41] Did Abraham's lack of attachment begin in early childhood or later when he had his life spared, and his brother Haran was sacrificed in his stead? Perhaps it begins around the time of the *Akeidah*.

According to Phyllis Trible, the *Akeidah*, first and foremost, tests Abraham's willingness to detach from his son so as to be able to turn to God:

> To attach is to practice idolatry. In adoring Isaac, Abraham turns from God. The test, then, is an opportunity for understanding and healing. To relinquish attachment is to discover freedom. To give up human anxiety is to receive divine assurance. To disavow idolatry is to find God.[42]

Thus, it would appear that God tempts Abraham to turn away from human attachment and choose divine attachment instead. Trible says this is to disavow idolatry, but surely Abraham's eagerness, to "over-worship" God, his excessive love of God, and his willingness to sacrifice his son to prove his love, may be considered a form of idolatry. On the one hand, Abraham wants to carry out what was a secure clear-cut command given by God, the source of all his security. Yet he is given a contradictory command not to sacrifice by the angel. Can this be another major factor contributing to his insecurity? There is no certainty when God's commands contradict conscience and morality. Abraham is faced with the fact that he must challenge God's commands, for they are contradictory. Both cannot be acted upon! If he totally disregards the first one, he is destroying a revelation from God, and breaching his own sense of security in God. If he totally disregards the second, he is violating his own sense of justice and ethics, and also ignoring a Divine revelation.[43]

God, too, appears to be insecure about Abraham's love. Why did he doubt him and put him to the test? If, as Judith Herman maintains, "traumatized people lose their trust in themselves, in other people, and in God," it is logical that God, who knows all about the trauma Abraham has experienced, would doubt Abraham's total faith in him. This would help to explain, why with the backing of Satan (as with Job), He would be tempted to put Abraham to the test.

According to Rashi, Abraham was ambivalent about whether to choose his love of his son or his love of God. It is clear that God wins out, but the cost is that he loses his son Isaac. According to Wendy Zierler, "The outcome of the *Akeidah* is that Isaac no longer appears in the story as Abraham's loved one. Perhaps even more startling, by the end of the story God is not Abraham's loved one either."[44] In the words of the poet, T. Carmi (1925–1994) in his poem "The Actions of the Fathers":

> "The voice from on high disappeared . . . And the voice within him (The only one left) said: Yes, you went from your land, from your homeland, the land of your father, and now, in the end, from yourself."

Until the momentous, horrific, command of the Akeidah, Abraham has only followed orders: *lech l'cha, asher arecha, sh'ma b'kolah, kah na,* etc. What Abraham suddenly understands, in his moment of truth, is that his unavailable mother figure, Amathlai, and three past father figures, Terah,

Nimrod, and God have sacrificed him to what they perceived as the greater cause. Terah, perhaps in protecting his status as an idol producer and for the love of his younger son, Haran, offered him as a sacrifice to Nimrod. Nimrod who literally wanted to burn him up and succeeded in doing so to his brother Haran, so that nothing was left of him, and who truly was an *olah*. Finally, God, who is so fixated on getting Abraham to accept the covenant and enter the promised land that he allows and even encourages Abraham to act dishonorably in leaving his father behind, using his wife Sarah, sending off Ishmael and Hagar at Sarah's re quest, and, most of all, in what has been referred to as the great testing of Abraham, telling him to sacrifice his remaining son in order to prove his obedience and faith. It is not clear what exactly is God's motivation, hence all the speculation over the generations.[45] However, Abraham's greatness is that he breaks his own cycle of abusive behavior by not following his previous role models and by not sacrificing Isaac. In Zornberg's words:

> "Abraham's work is to fathom the compulsions that led to filicide; to know in the present the full force of an experience of terror that lies enfolded in his past; to wake from his trance at the angel's call."[46]

God does not tell him to sacrifice the ram instead of Isaac (*ta chat b'no*). It is Abraham who SEES the ram and has a "click mo ment."[47] The Hebrew hints at this magnificently by using the word "*achar*" —in fact the cantillations, the Torah trope emphasize it (*ah ch-ah-ah-ar*).[48] There is another way! "*Vayisa Avraham et-einav, vayar, v'hinei, ayil ACHAR ne-echaz bas'vach b'karnav*" (Gen. 22:13).[49] Abraham makes a physical effort (*vayisa*) to raise his eyes; and then he SEES (*vayar*) an alternative (*achar*). There is another way. There is an out; he can truly see what is in front of him. Despite the hinted complication of the word (*bas'vach*, also a maze), it suddenly seems very simple. The ram (*ayil*) is for him. The "*hinei*" is representative of the two mentions of *hineini* (Here I am) in the text when he was willing to slavishly follow God's demand. Abraham is truly **here, now, in this new moment of truth,** as is the ram, the substitute for his son. He says, "I can stop the cycle of violence." Even though God has demanded proof of his love, he does not have to burn his son as a sacrifice. He has something else to offer, "*ACHAR*"; and this strange usage offers the reader closure by taking us back to the beginning of the story, *achar hadevorim ha-eleh*. It is something different, pointed to him by the Angel, something new that can lead into a more promising future — when there will be no more need to sacrifice. His greatness is that he does not have to be a repeat offender or a "serial" sacrificer.[50]

At the decisive moment when he SEES the ram, he, of his own volition, chooses to sacrifice it rather than his son. Abraham has two potential models of God. One is that of an unswerving worship in Maimonidean fashion: an obsessive worship of God as a lovesick man. But God does not tell him to worship Him that way, and Abraham chooses to follow the second command, the Angel's. The Angel, is the *ACHER*, the one who gives him a way out. He is also divine, but his message is that it is okay to sacrifice the ram, and not the son. So even though it is the only action Abraham takes on his own initiative with no specific command from God, it is because he has been able to decide on his own that some of God's commands do not have to be obeyed literally and can be carried out symbolically. The ram is *tachat b'no*, in place of his son, but that is Abraham's decision.[51]

His decision is not to inflict any more abuse, to realize that he can avoid repeating the abuse (the attempted filicide and fratricide) that was done to him in the past. He can say, I have choices, and this is what I choose. This is his real test, the one where he reaches deep into himself and with great courage defies God's temptation of him to repeat the pattern of abuse. This test he passes. He has avoided the temptation. He has achieved autonomy or agency. He has, in Herman's terminology, *recovered* from his trauma. He has chosen not to use the model of Maimonides' love, but one of his own choosing.

Herman suggests several steps of recovery—and as a psychiatrist, she would probably tell Abraham to go into analysis. According to her, for successful recovery it is necessary to go through three stages:

> We need to understand the past in order to reclaim the present and the future. An understanding of psychological trauma begins with rediscovering the past. The fundamental stages of recovery are:
>
> 1. Establishing safety
> 2. Reconstructing the traumatic story
> 3. Restoring the connection between the survivor and his/her community.[52]

One can argue that the angel, by offering an alternative, has created a safe environment for Abraham to choose his own model of worship. The midrash has helped him reconstruct the traumatic primordial story of the fire and the abuse he has suffered in his past history. Now all that remains is to restore the connection between himself and the community. It would seem that the latter is the easiest, because we all know that when he sends Eliezer off to find a wife for Isaac, he is ensuring a future connection between himself and the community. Yet, we cannot forget that the trauma he has inflicted on both of his sons has resulted in neither of them communicating with him for the rest of his life.

Part of this has to do with God's place in the previous scenario of abuse. Where is God in this scenario?[53] Has he retired totally from Abraham's life in disgust? I like the idea of the abusive God saying (like some parents), "Well I acknowledge my mistakes, I am doing *t'shuvah* and yes, I may have been abusive while you were growing up, but now you are a grown-up, you are a free person and I am proud of you, in that your first act was NOT to repeat the abuse that I have raised you with. And now you must take responsibility for your own actions."

Sadly, however, as a result of previous decisions, Abraham must still cope with the death of his wife (possibly his fault according to the midrash) and the disappearance of and non-communication with his son. These are not punishments, but consequences of previous abusive acts. What has been done cannot be undone, but the steps forward will hopefully teach the next generation how to behave—and note that both his sons do indeed come to bury him.

Abraham is a complicated human being, for morally speaking, he can argue with God over the fate of Sodom, yet can be morally neutral about sending Ishmael away and willing to slaughter Isaac. Once he has been willing to overstep the boundary of being a moral human, God never again addresses Abraham directly. Yet he does become more sensitive to others. He marries Keturah, has more children, provides for them during his lifetime, and sends Eliezer to arrange a marriage for Isaac and Rebekah. Thus, Abraham serves as a quintessential exemplar of humanity and the cycle of stories illustrates human complexity in dealing with trauma. In this sense, there is recovery.

Wilfred Owen (1893–1918), who died in action during World War I on November 4, 1918, hints in one of his most powerful poems, "The Parable of the Old Man and the Young," that Abraham actually "slew his son." Although there are midrashic sources that hint at Isaac's slaughter at his father's hand,[54] these are not mainstream, and so it is only fair to give Abraham the last word.

In two summations of his traumatic life, he says to Avimelech: "God **made** me wander from my father's house" (Gen. 20:13). וַיְהִי כַּאֲשֶׁר הִתְעוּ אֹתִי אֱלֹהִים֙ מִבֵּית אָבִי and later to Eliezer: "The LORD, the God of heaven, who **took me** from my father's house and from my native land" (Gen. 24:7). וַ אֱלֹהֵי הַשָּׁמַיִם אֲשֶׁר לְקָחַנִי מִבֵּית אָבִי֙ יְהוָה אָבִי֙ וּמֵאֶרֶץ מוֹלַדְתִּי.

There is poignancy here, for Abraham recognizes in retrospect that he was unable to feel mourning at the time. And this is part of his recovery when he says about himself that he had been forcibly taken from his father's home and his homeland by God, forced to wander and possibly be misled by God (hitu). For it was indeed God who took him from his birth land. This is the trauma from which Abraham almost never recovers. It is what is inscribed on his heart and possibly at the root of his tortuous love affair with God. This trauma, to a certain degree, is the one that we as a people, starting from Abraham through the aftermath of the Holocaust, have experienced, as one big tattoo inscribed, not only on our arms to identify ourselves, but as a trauma that, as in the prayer of the Sh'ma, has literally and figuratively been inscribed on our hearts and in our psyche. It is in the poet Haim Gouri's word, our "heritage," and the fact that according to him, while Abraham did not slaughter Isaac, in the end, we are "born with a knife in our hearts."[55] The continuing question is how to preserve memory of this suffering and at the same time recover from this very memory of our trauma. We need to figure out how to live lives that have meaning, nourish generations to come and help them in turn deal with the complexity of our lives and a seemingly remote and at times absent or quixotic God.

Notes

1. An earlier version of this paper was given at the Society of Biblical Literature International Meeting in the unit of Psychology and Bible in London, July 2011. A version of this article appears on the Web Edition of *Sh'ma: A Journal of Jewish Ideas,* dated September 19, 2011 (http://www.shma.com/2011/09/trauma and-recovery-abraham%e2%80%99s-journey-to-the-akedah/). I would like to express thanks to my three critical readers: Sidney Bloch, Michael Graetz, and Menorah Rotenberg.

2. Tikva Frymer Kensky, "*Akeda*: A View From the Bible," in *Beginning Anew: A Woman's Companion to the High Holidays,* ed. Judith Kates and Gail Twersky Reimer (New York: Touchstone, 1997), 144.

3. Wendy Zierler, "In Search of a Feminist Reading of the *Akedah*," *NASHIM: A Journal of Jewish Women's Studies and Gender Issues* (2005): 10.

4. Sören Kierkegaard, *Fear and Trembling*, trans. Walter Lowrie (Princeton: Princeton University Press, 1941). This material was prepared for Religion Online by Ted and Winnie Brock. 5. Cf. *Pirkei Avot* 5:3.

6. Jon Levenson in *The Death and Resurrection of the Beloved Son* (New Haven: Yale University Press, 1993) discusses the *Akeidah* in conjunction with the Book of Job.

7. See Yair Zakovitch, "The Exodus from Ur of the Chaldeans: A Chapter in Literary Archaeology," in *Ki Baruch Hu, Ancient Near Eastern, Biblical, and Judaic Studies in Honor of Baruch A. Levine*, ed. R. Chazan, W. W. Hallo, and L. H. Schiffman (Winona Lake, IN: Eisenbrauns, 1999), 429–39.

8. *B'reishit Rabbah* 38:13.

9. Aviva Gottlieb Zornberg, *The Murmuring Deep: Reflections on the Biblical Unconscious* (New York: Schocken Books, 2009), 147. 10. Zornberg, *Murmuring*, 189.

11. *P'sikta Zutarta* (*Lekach Tov*) Gen. 11, 28. I thank Michael Graetz for bringing this source to my attention.

12. Judith Herman, *Trauma and Recovery* (New York: Basic Books 1992, 1997). The 4th edition of *Diagnostic and Statistical Manual of Mental Disorders* (DSM) defi nes trauma occurring when "the per son experienced, witnessed, or was confronted with an event or events that involved actual or threatened death or serious injury, or threat to the physical integrity of self or others," and "the per son's response involved intense fear, helplessness, or horror." *Di agnostic and Statistical Manual of Mental Disorders*, 4th ed. (Washington, DC: American Psychiatric Association, 1994), 427, 428. 13. Herman, *Trauma and Recovery*, 33.

14. Ibid., 42–43.

15. Ibid., 56.

16. Ibid., 133.

17. *B'reishit Rabbah* 39:7.

18. "If such be the case, then Hegel is right when in his chapter on 'The Good and the Conscience,' he characterizes man merely as the particular and regards this character as 'a moral form of the evil' which is to be annulled in the teleology of the moral, so that the individual who remains in this stage is either sinning or subjected to temptation (*Anfechtung*). On the other hand, he is wrong in talking of faith, wrong in not protesting loudly and clearly against the fact that Abraham enjoys honor and glory as the fa ther of faith, whereas he ought to be prosecuted and convicted of murder." Kierkegaard, *Fear and Trembling*, 39.

19. BT *Sanhedrin* 89b; see also *Midrash Tanchuma* on *Lech L'cha* 10; Zornberg, *The Murmuring Deep*, 185.

20. For a discussion of this see Eugene Korn, Review Essay, "Windows on the World—Judaism Beyond Ethnicity: A Review of *Abraham's Journey* by Joseph B. Soloveitchik, edited by David Shatz, Joel B. Wolowelsky and Reuven Zeigler, and *Future Tense* by Rabbi Jonathan Sacks," *Meorot* 8 (Tishrei 5771/September 2010): 1–9.

21. See Naomi Graetz, "The Haftara Tradition and the Metaphoric Battering of Hosea's Wife," *Conservative Judaism* (Fall 1992): 29– 42; and Naomi Graetz, "Jerusalem the Widow," *Shofar* 17, no. 2 (Winter 1999): 16–24. Both articles are reprinted in Naomi Graetz, *Unlocking the Garden: A Feminist Jewish Look at the Bible, Midrash and God* (Piscataway, NJ: Gorgias Press, 2005).

22. Eric A. Seibert, *Disturbing Divine Behavior: Troubling Old Testament Images of God* (Minneapolis: Fortress, 2009), reviewed by John E. Anderson for *Review of Biblical Literature*, March 2, 2011, by the Society of Biblical Literature.

23. These thoughts came from a talk given by Kenneth Seeskin, "The Destructiveness of God," at the conference *Philosophical Investigation of the Hebrew Bible, Talmud and Midrash*, in Jerusalem, June 26–30, 2011, sponsored by The Shalem Center.

24. *B'reishit Rabbah* 39:1.

25. *Midrash Tanchuma Lech L'cha* 2.

26. Maimonides, *Hilchot T'shuvah*, chs. 2 and 3.

27. Aviva Gottlieb Zornberg develops this idea in her first book, *The Beginnings of Desire: Reflections on Genesis* (New York: Doubleday, 1996): 86– 93. However, Zornberg does not interpret this as pathology or abuse on the part of God.

28. *Love Does No Harm: Sexual Ethics for the Rest of Us* is the title of a book by Marie M. Fortune (New York: Continuum, 1995).

29. Zornberg, *Murmuring*, 178, writes that at the moment of the *Akeidah*, "Abraham's fear and desire make him *ripe* for the sacrificial act" (emphasis mine).

30. Herman, *Trauma and Recovery*, 137.

31. *B'reishit Rabbah* 39:8.

32. *B'reishit Rabbah* 39:9.

33. I would like to thank Menorah Rotenberg for this insight, personal communication.

34. Zornberg, *Murmuring*, 137.

35. Ibid., 188.

36. Herman, *Trauma and Recovery*, 133.

37. Ibid., 138. Note, since I am talking about Abraham, I have changed the gender from female to male.

38. B'reishit Rabbah 56:8.

39. John Bowlby, *Attachment and Loss*, vol. 1 (London: Hogarth, 1969), 194.

40. BT *Baba Batra* 91a.

41. Perhaps Haman's lack of confidence in himself, and the need to build himself up by destroying the "other," namely Mordecai and the Jews, is blamed on his mother's absence. But the similarity ends there, since Abraham's mother is associated with *har nevo* (and a clean animal) and Haman's mother with an unclean bird.

42. Phyllis Trible, "Genesis 22: The Sacrifice of Sarah," in *Women in the Hebrew Bible*, ed. Alice Bach (New York–London: Routledge, 1999), 278.

43. Unpublished paper by Rabbi Michael Graetz, "Abraham, the First Masorti Jew," published as a weekly column called *pina masortit* on ravnet for about ten years, date unknown.

44. Zierler, "Feminist Reading of the *Akedah*," 20–21. 45. Yair Lorberbaum gave a lecture as part of the *Tikvah Center for Law and Jewish Civilization Public Lecture Series at NYU*: "'Take now thy son, thine only son Isaac, whom thou lovest': Was Isaac Truly Beloved by Abraham? By God?" (November 30, 2010). In this talk he suggested that the source of all this testing is God's insecurity and jealousy of Abraham. He simply wants Abraham for himself and puts all sorts of obstacles in his path—including keeping him childless for so many years. And now when there is a child, he tries to get Abraham to get rid of it.

46. Zornberg, *Murmuring*, 200.

47. The expression "click moment" is usually associated with feminism. However, it probably originated with photography—the moment that the photographer frames the picture in her mind, using her eyes as the guide, which is the artistic moment of truth—then s/he clicks the button and preserves this vision for the future. It has been suggested to me that one can look at the three-day time frame of the journey to Moriah as a period that Abraham put to use by reflecting, confronting his past, and his lads, he is on his way to finding alternative behaviors to his abuse. It is true that one can argue that recovery is a process rather than a click moment, but I am not sure that Abraham has completely recovered (*nashuvah*); for his previous behavior has consequences for which he cannot totally make amends (*t'shuvah*). Furthermore the sparseness of the text and the leit motif of "seeing" that repeats itself over and over lend themselves to the click moment associated with both feminism and photography.

48. I am fully aware that I am taking liberties with my interpretation of *Achar*; but since the vocalization is the Masoretes' choice, one could also punctuate it and therefore pronounce it as *acher*. So I am doing it both ways!

49. *The Torah: A Women's Commentary*, 103, translates this as: "Abraham lifted his eyes: he now could see a ram [just] after it was caught by its horns in a thicket." The *Etz Hayim Torah and Commentary*, 120, translates this as: "When Abraham looked up, his eye fell upon a ram, caught in the thicket by its horns." In the commentary it writes: "'a ram behind [him]' or a 'ram, later [caught].'" It points to some manuscripts that say this is "'a single ram'" (*ayil echad*), which differs by only one similar-looking letter."

50. Ruhama Weiss uses the term in Hebrew "*oked sidrati*" (a serial sacrificer) to describe Abraham. See her article in Hebrew, "Blind Sarah" on the *Kolot* Web site, http://www.kolot.info.

51. See Michael Graetz, "Abraham, the First Masorti Jew," n. 43 above in this paper.

52. This is from a nice summary of Herman's *Trauma and Recovery* on the Web site http://www.uic.edu/classes/psych/psych270/ PTSD.htm.

53. See too my depiction of God (in the fi rst person) in the *Akedah* issue of *Sh'ma* (September 2011): 8.

54. See Shalom Spiegel, *The Last Trial*, trans. Judah Goldin (Philadelphia: JPS, 1967).

55. Haim Gouri, "Heritage":

> The ram came last of all.
> And Abraham did not know
> That it came to answer the boy's question—
> First of his strength when his day was on the wane.
> The old man raised his head.
> Seeing that it was no dream
> And that the angel stood there—
> The knife slipped from his hand.
> The boy, released from his bonds,
> Saw his father's back.
> Isaac, as the story goes, was not sacrificed.
> He lived for many years,
> Saw the good, until his eyes dimmed. But he bequeathed that hour
> to his descendants. They are born
> With a knife in their hearts.

Will The Real Hagar Please Stand Up?

Naomi Graetz

(Originally printed in Hagar: International Social Science Review 4:1 (2003): 213-219.)

Sarai, Abram's wife, had borne him no children. She had an Egyptian maidservant whose name was Hagar. And Sarai said to Abram, "Look, the LORD has kept me from bearing. Consort with my maid; perhaps I shall have a son through her." And Abram heeded Sarai's request. So, Sarai, Abram's wife, took her maid, Hagar the Egyptian — after Abram had dwelt in the land of Canaan ten years — and gave her to her husband Abram as concubine. He cohabited with Hagar and she conceived; and when she saw that she had conceived, her mistress was lowered in her esteem. And Sarai said to Abram, "The wrong done me is your fault! I myself put my maid in your bosom; now that she sees that she is pregnant, I am lowered in her esteem. The LORD shall decide between you and me!" Abram said to Sarai, "Your maid is in your hands. Deal with her as you think right." Then Sarai treated her harshly, and she ran away from her (Gen 16.1-6).

The story of Hagar is one of the most poignant and disturbing tales in the Bible. Throughout history, sensitive readers have been perturbed by the cynical exploitation of Hagar and her expulsion. The attitude toward the "other," which already began in biblical times, continues to plague us today; thus, it is important to study problematic texts, such as this one, in view of the fact that Sarai and Hagar's discord have reverberated until the present day.

Why this concern with the fate of Hagar? Why is her story important to us — especially since after the expulsion we do not hear of her again, at least in the biblical story? We do know

91

that her son, Ishmael, attends Abraham's funeral where he meets up with Sarah's son, Isaac. These concerns can be read into the Bible, the Hadith, and various midrashim. Often the midrash and the Hadith tend to resist the story in the Bible by devising a different plot, with a happy ending, or by showing the evil consequences of a particular act.

The Bible does not tell us anything of Hagar's origins. In Genesis 12.16 it is mentioned that Abram acquired some maidservants when he was in Egypt. The Koran does not mention her at all. According to one of the Muslim traditions,[1] Pharaoh gave to Sarai, Hagar, a Coptic slave-girl of his, because he was impressed with Sarai's goodness and beauty. Rashi writes that Hagar was a daughter of Pharaoh (Rashi on Gen 16.1). The midrash also identifies Keturah (Abraham's new wife in Gen 25.1 after Sarah dies) as Hagar. If Abraham had really divorced her (cast her out), he could not then have taken her as a wife, according to halakha. Thus, rabbinic tradition, in its positive reception of her, takes pains to show that Abraham did not "cast" her out; rather she was "sent" out. This would also apply to Ishmael. In redeeming Hagar, the rabbis trace her nobility and emphasize her qualities to justify her conversing freely with the angels and her attributing a name to God (el roi, God sees me). Following this same type of reasoning, Muslim tradition redeems Ishmael by telling how his father Abraham established the Kaaba in Mecca for him.

Some feminists depict Hagar as an object that is given by Sarai to Abraham. Although Sarai sees Hagar purely in terms of her breeding potential — like the handmaidens in Margaret Atwood's utopian novel, *The Handmaid's Tale* (1985)[2] — the

1 Al-Tabiri, "The History of al-Tabari," in William M. Brenner (tr.), *Prophets and Patriarchs* II (Albany: State University of New York Press, 1987): 62-63.
2 Margaret Atwood, *The Handmaid's Tale* (Toronto, Canada: McClelland and Stewart, 1985).

breeder rebels, in keeping with her status as Abraham's wife, not concubine. Other feminists see Hagar the bondmaid (*shifhah*) and/or slave (*amah*), as an exploited (second) wife, abused by those who are the first of our forefathers and foremothers. According to Phyllis Trible, Hagar is "one of the first females in scripture to experience use, abuse, and rejection."[3] She is a triple-fold alien: from her country, in her status, and in her sex.[4] She is an Egyptian maidservant living in Canaan; she is "single, poor and bonded."[5] She is a powerless object whose status is contingent on that of her mistress, Sarai, the wife of Abram.

[7]An angel of the Lord found her by a spring of water in the wilderness, the spring on the road to Shur, [8]and said, "Hagar, slave of Sarai, where have you come from, and where are you going?" And she said, "I am running away from my mistress Sarai." [9]And the angel of the Lord said to her, "Go back to your mistress, and submit to her harsh treatment." [10]And the angel of the Lord said to her, "I will greatly increase your offspring, and they shall be too many to count" (Gen 16.7-10).

The Bible's attitude towards Hagar is very sympathetic. In a story such as this—where Sarah calls the shots, Abraham displays ambivalence, God decides, and Hagar behaves passively—the focus would not normally be on Hagar after she is expelled. Instead, this silent woman becomes the center of the story, which turns into a story about her strength and feelings of pain and love for her child. Moreover, the angel clearly "cares" about her and talks to her, for she is a victim

---

3 Phyllis Trible, *Texts of Terror: Literary-Feminist Readings of Biblical Narratives* (Philadelphia: Fortress Press, 1984): 9.
4 Bruce Rosenstock, "Inner-Biblical Exegesis in the Book of the Covenant," *Conservative Judaism* (Spring 1992): 45 points out that the name Hagar may be a pun on *ger* (alien).
5 Phyllis Trible, *Texts of Terror: Literary-Feminist Readings of Biblical Narratives* (Philadelphia: Fortress Press, 1984): 10.

who is given an unequivocal message to remain a victim. It is as if he says to her, "Go back to this oppressive situation. Stay, don't run away. Your reward will be a son who will be a strong warrior." She is like a battered wife who runs away, yet doesn't know what to do with herself, thus returning to her original situation of learned helplessness.[6]

Despite this abusive situation, the angel of the Lord speaks to Hagar on two occasions. The first is when she is pregnant with Abram's seed and Sarai is threatened by Hagar's new position. Sarai was tacitly allowed by Abram to do with Hagar as she pleased. "Your maid is in your hands. Deal with her as you think right" (Gen 16.6).

The midrash, perhaps aware of the unfairness in this, reveals a shade of ambivalence on Abram's part:

> Said he: "I am constrained to do her neither good nor harm [since she is now my wife]. It is written, Thou shalt not deal with her as a slave, because thou hast humbled her (Deut xxi, 14): after we have vexed her, can we now enslave her again? I am constrained to do her neither good nor harm" (*Gen. Rabba* 45:6).

> The midrash goes on to shift the blame to Sarai making her totally responsible for the physical and mental violence inflicted upon Hagar.
> R. Abbah said: She restrained her from cohabitation.
> R. Berekiah said: She slapped her face with a slipper.
> R. Berekiah said in R. Abbah's name: She bade her carry her water buckets and bath towels to the baths.
> (*Gen. Rabba* 45:6)

---

6 Lenore Walker, a forensic psychologist, in *The Battered Woman* (Harper & Row, 1979) relied heavily on the concept of learned helplessness to support the view of battered women's syndrome.

In light of the fact that Hagar had the status of a wife, Sarah, in giving her menial work, both mistreated and humiliated her.

Hagar is not encouraged to fight for her freedom; rather it is assumed that she remain in her servant status. She is advised to stay where she is and suffer for the sake of her future child: Accept the abuse now, because your own life is of no intrinsic worth. You live for the sake of your son; you are the caretaker of his future.

When Hagar has her son, Ishmael, Sarah[7] is again incensed and this time tells Abraham to "cast out that slave-woman and her son…" (21.10). This time, as Trible points out, "Hagar has lost her name… Moreover, the absence of dialogue continues to separate the females. Inequality, opposition, and distance breed violence."[8]

Although the matter distressed Abraham greatly, not because of Hagar, but because it "concerned a son of his" (Gen 21.11) God tells him not to be …distressed over the boy or your slave; whatever Sarah tells you, do as she says… As for the son of the slave-woman, I will make a nation of him, too, for he is your seed (Gen 21.12-13).

Thus, the "son" becomes "a boy" and "Hagar" becomes a "slave." As Trible puts it, "if Abraham neglected Hagar, God belittles her."[9]

In these biblical texts, God identifies with the oppressor, not with the oppressed. God and Abraham are accomplices in the

---

7 Sarai gets her name changed to Sarah in Gen 17.15 and Abram to Abraham in Gen 17.5.

8 Phyllis Trible, *Texts of Terror: Literary-Feminist Readings of Biblical Narratives* (Philadelphia: Fortress Press, 1984): 13.

9 Idem: 22.

decision to cast out the object, the slave-woman of no account. Abraham cares only about his seed, his son, not about the woman. It is Sarah who cares about being supplanted and who initiates the act. It would appear that the Bible also sympathizes with Sarah's plight when it writes that it is a "loathsome" situation when "a slave girl supplants her mistress" (Prov 30.23).

What does it mean that the Angel sees the suffering of the despised woman, the Egyptian stranger (*ha-ger*)? What are the parallels between his promises to her and to Abraham? Compare the fact that the Angel of God speaks twice to Hagar and only once to Sarah. The rabbis themselves wonder at the fact that God speaks to Hagar and explain it by saying that "Abraham's household was used to seeing angels up close because of his close relationship with God." Is God's blessing of Ishmael a fair distribution of goods between Abraham's two sons?

It is not only Hagar who is damaged; her child suffers as well, both physically and spiritually. Hints of this can be read in the blessing (or perhaps curse) given to Hagar by the divine messenger:

> Behold, you are with child
> And shall bear a son;
> You shall call him Ishmael,
> For the Lord has paid heed to your suffering.
> He shall be a wild ass of a man;
> His hand against everyone,
> And everyone's hand against him;
> He shall dwell alongside of all his kinsmen
> (Gen 16.11-12).

Ishmael has witnessed that God had not "paid heed to [her] suffering" and that, in fact, she had been abused by all those close to her. It is likely that he will grow up with a chip on his shoulder, perceiving that "everyone's hand [is] against him" and that "his hand [will be] against everyone." He will also become an oppressor, when he gets the chance, even against the people of Israel.

What does biblical law have to say about the expulsion of Ishmael?

The laws of the Torah do not permit parents, or even legal authorities, to expel a son or daughter from the home for any reason. According to the Torah, nobody can divest an offspring of his legal status in the household to which he belongs. This was not the practice among other peoples in the ancient Near East: Various codices and ancient legal documents, some even predating the time of Abraham, attest that expelling one's offspring from the parents' home, i.e., divesting a child of his legal status in his father's house, was a legitimate legal procedure in cases of offenses committed against the parents. While the Torah was not lenient about the punishment of a child who committed an offense against his parents—a child who struck or cursed his parents could be sentenced to death, if proven guilty—nevertheless he could not be banished for delinquent behavior.[10]

Hence, Abraham's casting out of Hagar and Ishmael is problematic. Ishmael is a legal son of Abraham's whom he circumcised at age thirteen. Sarah's words, "Cast out that slave-woman and her son, for the son of that slave shall not share in the inheritance with my son Isaac" (21.10), make it obvious that she thought he did have rights to Abraham's inheritance by virtue of being Abraham's son.

---

10 Joseph Fleischman *"Parashat Vayera* 5760/1999, The Expulsion of Ishmael," (Bar Ilan University, Weekly Internet Sermons).

To make this illegality more palatable, traditional midrash demonizes Ishmael to illustrate how his action against Isaac was worthy of his being demoted as a legal heir and deserving of exile. The pretext that Sarah used to expel Ishmael was that he was making "sport" with (*metzahek*) Isaac. The midrash says that this refers to his immorality and Sarah's prophetic vision that he would ravish maidens and seduce married woman in the future (*Gen. Rabba* 53:11). Maimonides comments that God saw Hagar's affliction and gave her a son who was destined to be a lawless person. This contradicts the biblical text which states that Abraham loved Ishmael too (Gen 17.18; 21.11, 26) and that Ishmael was blessed in his ways (17.20) and God was with the lad (21.20). Surely the bible would not have said this about someone who was destined to be a lawless person.

There are those who identify the victimization of Hagar as a prefiguration of Israel's enslavement in Egypt. According to Trible, Hagar, unlike Israel,

> ... experiences exodus without liberation, revelation without salvation, wilderness without covenant, wanderings without land, promise without fulfillment, and unmerited exile without return. This Egyptian slave woman is stricken, smitten by God, and afflicted for the transgressions of Israel.[11]

Following Trible's insights one step further, I would argue that Hagar, the suffering slave woman, serves as a prototype for the metaphor of Israel as the suffering, mistreated wife of God.[12]

---

11 Phyllis Trible, *Texts of Terror: Literary-Feminist Readings of Biblical Narratives* (Philadelphia: Fortress Press, 1984): 28.
12 For an expansion of this point see the previous article in this book "God is to Israel as Husband is to Wife" on page 69.

In the Islamic versions of the expulsion of Hagar and Ishmael there are many expansions on the original biblical text to emphasize Ishmael's mother's extraordinary stamina and dedication as a mother. In one tradition, Abraham goes with them as far as Mecca and then returns home. When she asks, "To whom are you leaving us?" He replies "to Allah." When her water is used up, she goes down a mountain and runs back and forth seven times between the mountains of Safa and Marwa, before she hears from the angel Gabriel. He causes water to gush forth from the earth (the sacred well of Zamzum) and this attracts first birds and then people who join her and form a community. Muslim pilgrims traditionally imitate Hagar's distress by encircling these sacred spots. After Ishmael's mother dies, Abraham returns several times to visit his son and the relationship continues. He checks to see if Ishmael has married a suitable wife by testing them with riddles (2.127 *Sahih Bukhari* 4.584). Abraham and Ishmael together build the temple in Mecca and place in it the black stone.

CONCLUSION

One father, two wives, two sons, and two different traditions emerge from this original biblical tale. Why was Abraham destined to have the two sons? Wouldn't it have been much simpler if there were only one? Every child with a brother or sister fantasizes about being an only child. What does it mean when our tradition tells us that one child is predestined to cause the other trouble? Moreover, why does God cause suffering to both their mothers? There are no real answers to these questions. Perhaps it is only an articulation of reality: this is the way of the world; very few of us are "lucky" enough to be an only child; most of us have to learn how to live with the other. The problem with this is that often we find "the other" too difficult to deal with and we end up demonizing him or her[13] to keep them at bay and justify our treatment of those who are different.

Issues such as these become even more complicated when God is introduced into the discussion, and we are taught that the Deity has commanded us to behave in such a fashion, that is, to cast out the one who is not the favorite son. Sarah and Hagar's enmity had repercussions that we, the heirs of Ishmael and Isaac, still suffer from. When one is asked, "where have we come from" and "where are we going to," I suggest being prepared with the following answer: Our mutual past history may have limited and enslaved us, but now it is time to move beyond the past.

---

13 For instance there was Rabbi Ovadia Yosef's sermon which compared Arabs to snakes that should all be annihilated. In this utterance, Yosef, once known as a political dove, denounced Barak for "running after" the Palestinians. "Why are you bringing them close to us?" he asked. "You bring snakes next to us. How can you make peace with a snake?" Dismissing the Arabs as "Ishmaelites," he added for bad measure: "They are all accursed, wicked ones. They are all haters of Israel. It says in the Gemara that the Holy One, Blessed be He, is sorry he created these Ishmaelites" *The Jewish Journal of Greater Los Angeles* (August 11, 2000).

Dvar Torah for Rosh Hashana

Hannah M. Heller

I often complain about the clothing styles available to women. So many of them don't have pockets. I like to put my keys in a pocket when I go for a walk or carry a few things I need without having to shlep a bag.

A pocket allows us to carry things as we go from one place to the other. What happens if you put too many things in your pockets? Your load gets heavy, and walking is more difficult. You also might tear the pocket. When Passover time comes, you can often find old candy wrappers and other things in pockets that you need to get rid of before the holiday.

When we leave the old year and enter the new year it is important to avoid being weighed down by our actions of the past. We don't have to carry these overflowing pockets into the new year. In order to feel that G-d will grant us a good year ahead, we need to develop the confidence that we are worthy of forgiveness. If we keep thinking about our past mistakes, we will have a hard time "emptying our pockets" of the burdens that hinder our process of *"Teshuva,"* repentance, returning to G-d.

Mossy Wittenberg notes that unlike Passover, when we remember the event of leaving Egypt, on Rosh Hashana we are not commanded to remember a specific event. We commanded to *remember Who We Are and To What We Belong.* Since G-d knows and cares about everyone, no one can hide away when it comes to reconnecting with Him. On the High Holy Days, what we feel is out in the open, not hidden in the pockets of our clothing. Some people have the custom of turning their pockets inside out when they say Tashlich on Rosh Hashana to show that we are *"emptying our sins"* into the water. In our Rosh Hashana prayers, we have a blessing that ends with G-d being *"zocher habrit,"* mindful of the covenant, remembering the special relationship He has with each one of us.

The Talmud gives three descriptions of how we all come before G-d on Rosh Hashana. The Hebrew phrase is "Bnei Maron," literally like sheep being counted. Rabbi Nechemiah Coopersmith relates that there are three explanations. One is that "All people pass before G-d like sheep being led through a narrow door and counted one by one. Another interpretation is that we each pass before G-d as if we were on a steep and narrow mountain where we have to walk single file. A third explanation is that we pass before G-d like soldiers in King David's army in single file, on our way to war. When we consider ourselves like the sheep being counted, we come to realize that if we are being counted, we are considered valuable and important. When we talk about walking the steep and narrow mountain in single file, we note that we are all alone, with nowhere to hide. There is no one else, no big society, no excuse in social media. It's only the real you, being all you can be, away from the distractions that might keep you from getting to know yourself better. When we say we are like King David's soldiers, we are comparing ourselves to those who are strong and mighty. Each soldier in this army had a unique mission and each person contributed with a different strength.

On Rosh Hashana we stand before G-d and we reconnect with all our dreams and goals. G-d wants a relationship with us. We have to allow ourselves to communicate with G-d who is rooting for us to do great things.

Rabbi Yissocher Frand relates that on Rosh Hashana anything can happen, and life can change for the better. It is determined what kind of year we will have, how much money we will earn and what challenges we will face. What happened in the past year is over and we start anew. Our circumstances can change. G-d can grant us more income, better health and strong connections with family and friends. If you have been successful in life until now, continuing this success is not a guarantee. Connecting with G-d and praying for continued prosperity is part of Rosh Hashana davening.

Rabbi Toba Spitzer shares writer Joan Wickersham's story of someone going on a trip 30 years ago before we had electronic devices to guide us.

> "As we set off on this journey, we don't entirely lack a map. We know where we've been and hopefully have some sense of where we would like to get to. But the road itself lies before us, and who knows what mysterious signs might appear along the way? The challenge is to relish, not fear, the sense of openness, of not knowing, remaining open to whatever might come."

I don't know if more clothing designers will include pockets for women, but if they do, I will be very happy. Regardless of whether or not you have physical pockets in your clothes, let go of the mental baggage that has weighted you down, hiding as though it was buried deeply in a pocket. Get in touch with who you are as you strengthen your relationship with G-d and with our fellow human beings.

Shana Tova. Ktiva V'Chatima Tova. May you all be inscribed for a good year.

Tashlich
Susan Hornstein, Ph.D.

It was the first time I'd ever felt anything at *Tashlich*. Anything relevant to the ritual, that is. Usually I feel joy, at seeing people from different Jewish sub-communities streaming toward the river in our beautiful park, at sitting on my front steps watching the procession, at going to the park on Rosh Hashana afternoon. But of course, none of those things felt normal at all that year, 5781, better known as 2020, during the COVID-19 pandemic. Lacking the structure of a communal meeting time, I didn't even go on Rosh Hashana, rather I stopped by the river on one of my daily walks around the park during the following week. Even those walks hadn't always been daily, and had only become part of my routine when time stood still that year.

In previous years I'd always bristled a little at the ritual of *Tashlich*. It felt too literal. Too made-up. Too complicated, telling the kids that we don't have the custom of throwing bread, and that anyway feeding the ducks on Yom Tov wasn't ok even though all their friends were doing it. Too pat. Throw the sins away, toss them in water, any water, even a well. What could that do for me?

But that year, standing alone by the river, I started to wonder. What would it mean to let go? To allow my sins to float out of me and dissolve, to be cancelled out by the vastness of the world. Could the universe absorb my guilt and leave me a little lighter?

Then again, we unwittingly release all sorts of things into the universe, and the result is rather bad. The universe can't bear much more of our emissions, our unthinking consumerism, our disregard for her integrity.

The High Holy Day prayers refer to the fear of God applying to all God's creations, animate and inanimate. And that when all the creations of the world unite in awe of God, then all will do God's will with one united heart. While I was reciting this prayer, I was reminded of our interdependence, how we all rely on one another. All people rely on each other to keep each other safe and healthy. People rely on the natural world, and the natural world relies on people, to steward each other and keep each other sustainable.

Our sages tell us that we should always regard ourselves as if we have a ledger consisting of exactly half demerits and half merits. This way, every action we take can have the effect of shifting our balance one way or the other. Moreover, we are told to regard the whole world as hanging in that very balance, so that every action we take could shift the world toward good or evil.

So, what could it mean to release my sins into the water? Why should I need to look at water to cleanse myself of guilt? Outdoors, that year, I felt for the first time that my *teshuva* process was connected to the world around me. Not just to the other people in my community, but to the water, and the air, and God's creations both animate and inanimate. Maybe the world is big enough to absorb my guilt, like a mother who is big enough to swallow you up in her hug. Maybe I need to accumulate a little less guilt in the coming year, so as not to tip the world's delicate balance too far. Maybe I can strike a balance between vigilance and allowing myself to let go. For now, I think I'll just cast my bread on the water.

Nitzavim: Still in Love?
Rabbanit Bracha Jaffe

Parashat Nitzavim, which is always read right before Rosh Hashana, describes a scene where **all** of Bnei Yisrael are standing together as Moshe begins to wind down his farewell speech to them. [Deut 29:9]

אַתֶּם נִצָּבִים הַיּוֹם כֻּלְּכֶם לִפְנֵי ה' אֱלֹקֵיכֶם

"You are standing today **all of you** before the LORD your God"

Moshe explains **why** they are all standing there [Deut 29:11]

לְעָבְרְךָ, בִּבְרִית ה' אֱלֹקֶיךָ--וּבְאָלָתוֹ: אֲשֶׁר ה' אֱלֹקֶיךָ, כֹּרֵת עִמְּךָ הַיּוֹם.

"So that you should enter into the **covenant** of the LORD your God--and into God's oath--which the LORD your God is making with you today."

Rav Shneur Zalman - the author of the *Tanya* asks this question:

> Why did Hashem need to make a **new** covenant with the Israelites, just as they were about to enter the Land of Israel? Wasn't the treaty they made at Har Sinai enough?

Explains the *Ba'al HaTanya*: The *Brit* - covenant - between two lovers, is not for the time when their love and affection is strong and sure. It is for the uncertain times, when things may feel rocky, and the original love weakens as circumstances change and life intervenes. Thus, they can remember the treaty and fall back on it to reawaken their feelings and trust in one another.

In the desert, while Moshe was alive, the Israelites lived a supernatural life with daily miracles such as a traveling well and *maan* that fell from the heavens. In the Land of Israel, there was plowing, planting, and harvesting. Anxiety about rainfall and fear of settling the land might create distance and a lessening of their love for God. This *Brit* - this covenant - was a promise made when the love and connection to God was robust and strong, promising that it would endure forever like "a tent peg stuck deep in the earth" in the words of Rav Shneur Zalman.

Let us remember this teaching when our own relationships - with God, with our partners, with our friends - feel like the honeymoon period is over and it's time to wash the dishes and do the laundry, which can cause friction. That is when we can fondly and lovingly recall the caring connection and perhaps unspoken *Brit* that brought us together and rekindle our love for each other and for God.

Our Four Sacred New Years

Rabbanit Nomi Kaltmann
Edited by Ronda Angel Arking

(previously published on Jofa.org)

Rosh Hashana, the Jewish new year that takes place each year in Tishrei involves an abundance of ritual and preparation. We blow the shofar; we eat symbolic foods; we prepare ourselves for long hours of communal prayer. We celebrate the ushering in of the Jewish new year with festive meals and reflecting on our conduct over the past year. Together with our families, we eat pomegranates and other delicacies and collectively celebrate making it to another year together. L'hayyim, we all say!

The start of a new year holds much special symbolism. Across cultures around the world, the new year is often ushered in with parties and celebrations. If new years have been happening since the onset of calendars, why do they generate such exuberant reactions each year? Such celebrations must be tied to a deeper, intrinsic human need that speaks to something deeper within ourselves.

After all, each year planning a celebration means that humans choose to invest energy and resources, as well as often identify a new set of goals for the year ahead. These rituals take time and motivation and speak to a deeper need, one that links the new year to the human desire for renewal and improvement. Judaism breaks the universal mold of a new year's celebration by offering a model of multiple new years. Rosh Hashana is one of four annual "new year's celebrations," listed in the Mishnah, each with its own importance and representation:

אַרְבָּעָה רָאשֵׁי שָׁנִים הֵם. בְּאֶחָד בְּנִיסָן רֹאשׁ הַשָּׁנָה לַמְּלָכִים וְלָרְגָלִים. בְּאֶחָד בֶּאֱלוּל רֹאשׁ הַשָּׁנָה לְמַעְשַׂר בְּהֵמָה. רַבִּי אֶלְעָזָר וְרַבִּי שִׁמְעוֹן אוֹמְרִים, בְּאֶחָד בְּתִשְׁרֵי. בְּאֶחָד בְּתִשְׁרֵי רֹאשׁ הַשָּׁנָה לַשָּׁנִים וְלַשְּׁמִטִּין וְלַיּוֹבְלוֹת, לַנְּטִיעָה וְלַיְרָקוֹת. בְּאֶחָד בִּשְׁבָט, רֹאשׁ הַשָּׁנָה לָאִילָן, כְּדִבְרֵי בֵית שַׁמַּאי. בֵּית הִלֵּל אוֹמְרִים, בַּחֲמִשָּׁה עָשָׂר בּוֹ:

The four new years are: On the first of Nisan, the new year for the kings and for the festivals; On the first of Elul, the new year for the tithing of animals; in the first of Tishrei. On the first of Tishrei, the new year for years, for the Sabbatical years and for the Jubilee years and for the planting and for the vegetables. On the first of Shevat, the new year for the trees, these are the words of the House of Shammai; The House of Hillel says, on the fifteenth thereof. (Mishnah Rosh Hashana 1:1)

Let's start by unpacking the four different new years celebrations. The first of Nissan is considered the new year for counting the reign dates of the Jewish kings of ancient Israel. It also symbolizes the first month of the Jewish calendar, as festivals are counted from the first of Nissan onward. This date is intrinsically tied to the freedom of the Jewish people from slavery in Egypt, and commemorates the anniversary of our peoplehood. By marking the reign of the king at this time it reminds us that we are marking our exodus and emergence as a people from slavery to peoplehood and to self-rule.

The second Jewish New Year is the first of Elul. According to the Mishnah, this is the new year for providing agricultural ma'aser (tithes). This was an important time in the calendar, like yearly tax accounting periods, where one was obligated to take stock of their produce and pay their required donations. This also marked an opportunity where one could account for their blessings, their produce, and their successes (as well as areas for improvement!), a mere few months after the first of Nissan.

This leads to the third new year's celebration — just one month later — Rosh Hashana on the first of Tishrei. This is the anniversary of the creation of the world and the birth of humans. It celebrates the creation of people into the dynamic world that God created. It is also used for calculating the Sabbatical and Jubilee years, which play important roles in Jewish ritual.

The fourth and final new year is Tu Bishvat, the fifteenth day of Shevat, which celebrates the new year of the trees. It marks the date from which the age of trees is determined, meaning the biblical waiting periods for eating from agricultural crops begins on this date.

The fact that Judaism recognizes that there are four new years within each calendar year is revelatory. It shows that Judaism marks time differently, that the chance to start afresh is not a one-time opportunity. With each new year bringing its unique rituals and obligations, Judaism emphasizes the possibility of a second (and third, and fourth!) chance.

The Mishnah recognizes that each of these time periods brings forth a unique opportunity for marking an occasion and for renewal. Each of these sacred time periods offers us the opportunity to express our humanity and desire for constant improvement.

We join together in Nissan to mark out peoplehood from the depths of slavery. When we mark the first of Elul, we recognize the tithing and tax systems that keep society running. And when we mark the birth of humanity and the birthday of the trees we acknowledge the duality of our system, one in which humans must abide by the laws of nature in order to celebrate the hope and creativity that God has allowed to flourish in this world.

As humans we all have an innate desire for belonging, to find meaning in our rituals and the traditions that allow us to find something greater in the world around us.

And yet, each time we gather together to mark a new time period, be it a birthday or a new year, we are finding the sacred in the ritual. We mark the occasions by gathering to acknowledge the changes in the world around us; to contemplate the way time is passing us by; and to ponder the meaning of what this passage of time means for our individual lives.

Judaism, with its rhythms and calendars, allows humans the opportunity to reach for balance. Multiple new years embedded into our calendar offer opportunities to find meaning with the different seasons of our lives. This calendar reflects a vision that God has for each one of us, namely, that our lives are not static and that each time offers its own opportunity for introspection and ability for self-expression. And this is precisely why the new year, represents our desire for renewal and improvement. We want to be better. We want to have some control over our upcoming lives, because if the last year has taught us anything, it is that the future is highly unpredictable. We therefore use the sacred times set by God to resolve to do better. We take the opportunities to recommit ourselves. And in this way, we take back control over our lives with the rededication of our hearts and minds to God's sacred obligations.

Hayom Harat Olam: Of Children, Slaves and Choices

Joelle Keene

You are standing by your seat with your eyes closed: it's Rosh Hashana and the shofar is sounding. It wails and blasts and you're filled with spirit and awe. It goes on forever – and you partly want it to go on forever, because it takes you to a place of such gratefulness and majesty. And you partly want it to end, because it makes you so uncertain and afraid.

Then, finally, silence – just for a moment. And then, a prayer that is said only now: Hayom Harat Olam.

Hayom harat olam literally means today is the "conception" or "pregnancy" of the world. The idea, according to Rabbi Adin Steinsaltz, is that the year is a kind of embryo, all its DNA already present, the future already created, and we know it is there but we cannot yet see it, it has not yet developed to a point where it is visible. We don't know what it's going to be like.

An embryo presumes the presence of parents, and sure enough God is depicted in this text partly as a parent -- but only partly. Pleading for a favorable judgement, the prayer goes on to say, "If as children, have compassion as a father has compassion for his sons; if as slaves, our eyes are raised and fixed on You until You show us favor."

So, we are not only children, but slaves. What is the difference between these two? One, it seems to me, is that a child is being trained to choose what is right in the future, when he or she will have free will, many, many choices and much responsibility. A slave, however, has no choices and does not anticipate them.

Yet both of these describe our relationship with God: on the one hand, we have free will, and we choose to follow God's laws because we understand that they are for our and society's benefits. On the other, we have no choice; in the case of *chukim,* or even of laws that bother us or that we find difficult, we must follow them anyway. God created the world; we are in awe of Him; we obey. He teaches us like a parent, with Torah and the particular gifts and challenges of our lives. But we are in awe, and we know He has the last word. Along with so many other things, He is truly the ultimate Master.

Perhaps this dichotomy finds its way into the climax of the Rosh Hashana service because the challenge of free will vs. our commanded state and role is the crux of our religious struggle. On the one hand, we want to do what's good and right, and we are grateful for God's instruction. But we are also God's slaves -- commanded and not looking forward to a day when we can do whatever we want; there is no such day coming. On Pesach, we celebrate "freedom," being free to follow God. But Rosh Hashana is the holiday of *malchut* -- when we accept God's *kingship.*

Kingship and "subject-hood" can be difficult **themes/constructs/paradigms** for Jews raised in a modern democracy -- especially in a country which was formed for the purpose of throwing off a king's power and which famously has replaced that template with government by consent of the governed. We naturally push back against it; I personally find that part of the liturgy difficult every time, even in Avinu Malkeinu.

But in fact, we *are* subjects of the King. The king of kings -- of parents, of presidents and governors, of bosses, of corporate leaders, of cultural icons. Hayom Harat Olam says: *Please do both* – see us as dependents and love us, and when You can't, show us favor anyway. This relationship is -- complicated. And it's obvious that You have the last word.

Rabbi Jonathan Sacks affirms this. Quoting Rav Soloveitchik in the new Koren Machzor, he says that on Rosh Hashana we ourselves crown God as king, because there can be no king without subjects. Perhaps Hayom Harat Olam reminds us that not only are we subject to God's judgements, compassion and commands, but we are the followers whose fealty actually makes Him the king! Kingship is complex and our feelings are too; therefore, we appeal to God on many levels, trying to grasp (and show that we have grasped) the complexity of what is going on here: God is our master; God is our parent; and God is our also consent-of-the-governed - chosen King.

So again and again, throughout the holiday and especially when the shofar is sounded, we crown Him our king -- because we want to be subject specifically and most profoundly to Him, and really only to Him. He governs absolutely, He governs with compassion, and He governs with our consent.

It's complicated -- and it's part of what makes Rosh Hashana so rich, and the shofar-blowing so mind-blowing, and what fills us with hope even though we are partly scared and overcome by the shofar's sounds. So just as the echoes of the *tekiah* fade in the room, we sing: Today the year is an embryo, we know it's complicated, we understand who we are and who You are, and we therefore appeal to You on all these levels, understanding that Your role is complex beyond anything we can fathom.

And from there we go back into the liturgy of the day, hopefully even more than before on the same page with the One who is judging us at that very time, on that very day, moment by moment.

The Stolen Shofar

Rabba Sara Hurwitz,
Maharat President and Co-Founder

There's a key difference between the shofar and other ritual objects: The mishnah in Sukkot and elsewhere clearly states that a stolen object cannot be used to perform the ritual. A Lulav Gazul (stolen lulav) (or etrog or tefillin or even matza) are not considered to be kosher if it's stolen because:

> מצוה הבאה בעבירה
> a mitzvah that came about from a sin cannot fulfill the obligation.

It is strange that the Mishnayot in Mesechet Rosh Hashana are silent on the topic of a stolen shofar. Although you might assume that a stolen shofar also cannot be used, the Rambam in Mishneh Torah, Hilchot Shofar (1:3) teaches the opposite - a stolen shofar *can* indeed be used. A surprise twist!

> שׁוֹפָר הַגָּזוּל שֶׁתָּקַע בּוֹ יָצָא שֶׁאֵין הַמִּצְוָה אֶלָּא בִּשְׁמִיעַת הַקּוֹל ... וְאֵין בַּקּוֹל דִּין גָּזֵל
> A stolen shofar that a person has blown has fulfilled [the obligation]. For the commandment is only listening to the sound.... and there is no law of theft with sound. Sound cannot be stolen.

Using a stolen shofar is kind of insane, especially when you consider that our rabbinic tradition placed so much emphasis on the shofar itself. There are specific laws around which animal a shofar can come from, whether it can be bent or straight, gold plated, or if a cracked shofar can still be used. Clearly the shofar as an object, the way in which it is constructed, is significant enough for our tradition to mandate all these laws. And yet as long as it is bent, made from a ram, not split along the entire length in half, or gold plated at the

116

mouth of the shofar we may use a stolen shofar? The only indication that a stolen shofar may be problematic is from the Magen Avraham (586:4), who suggests that you shouldn't make a bracha over it!

I have to say that if I knew that I was listening to the tekiyot of a stolen shofar I would not feel like I was achieving the purpose and goals of Rosh Hashana -- of coronating God as king and thinking about the shofar as a messenger for our tefilot and for remembering our past.

The Ra'avad (Laws of Shofar 1:3, based on the Yerushalmi Sukkah 3:1) explains that Rosh Hashana is defined as "yom teruah" a day of sounding the shofar, whose very essence is to stir us and awaken us to think about our deeds. And what is the one thing that prevents us from moving forward? When we get stuck in the past -- when we can't let go of past iniquities and memories -- we are prevented from changing. Perhaps the stolen shofar is a reminder that the past needs to stay in the past if we are to ever move forward and change.

It is Rambam's simple answer that I find most compelling. For the Rambam, the Shofar is all about the *sound*. All the halakhot that make the shofar kosher are intended to preserve the pure sound of the shofar. A cracked, straight, or gold-plated shofar would alter the sound. Since the sound is still intact, despite the fact that it is stolen, it accomplishes the purpose of the mitzvah.

This is where our focus must lie. The message of the stolen shofar, the reason why it is kosher, is to underscore that the object does not matter. I imagine that if today's ba'al tekiya was indeed using a stolen shofar, that's all we would want to talk about. Why did he steal it? Who did he steal it from? Will he return it? But those would be the wrong questions. Our attention may be drawn to the shiny object right before us because it is human nature to be enthused and excited by the austere beautiful shofar, or the ba'al tekiyah himself, but if we notice only the shofar or the person, we are missing the point of the mitzvah.

There is actually a name for the phenomenon of being distracted and focusing on the wrong thing: shiny object syndrome (SOS), a psychological concept where people focus on whatever is most current or trendy. In fact, people who face a fear of missing out (FOMO) are especially susceptible as newer shinier objects cause distraction, cloud judgment and cause loss of focus.

We worry about the thing that shouts loudest at us in the media. Our attention is short and must be held by dramatic images. We are drawn to the heart wrenching images of people dying from COVID or the damage from a hurricane or the pictures of war or the headline about abortion in Texas. And we *must* care about these things. But these dramatic headlines will disappear, and in their wake, there will be individuals still picking up the pieces after suddenly losing a loved one or who struggle from long COVID or there will be a woman who no longer has the right to decide what to do with her body. For every headline there are the individual, more quiet tragedies that don't make news. Even our own everyday challenges get lost in the shuffle.

Awaken, says the shofar. Pay no attention to the vessel even if it is stolen. Pay attention to the sound that emanates that is calling to your soul.

it is easy to become mired in the smallness of the shiny objects. There are so many crises and events that we must pay attention to. Sometimes I wonder how we can even get out of bed with the crushing sensation of it all. Yet, my challenge this year is to cut through the noise and focus on what matters. Not on whether the shofar is stolen or not.

The sound of the shofar is a tool for what we can achieve and accomplish in the world. So, this year when I hear the *shevarim truah* I will acknowledge and cry and mourn for all that is broken. For the things I am struggling with in my life. For the struggles of our society and world. I will allow the sadness to wash over me even if I can't fix it all today.

And then, I will feel emboldened by the strong, sure sounds of the tekiyot. The sounds that bookend the sadness and I will listen for the song of triumph, hearing that there will be days ahead that are filled with joy and celebration and hope.

And the familiar sounds of the shofar will keep me focused on what really counts.

Rosh Hashana 5783
Rabbanit Yael Keller

Shana Tova. It is wonderful to be here, welcoming in the New Year together. Over Rosh Hashana, we celebrate with sweetness. We taste the sweetness of honey and apples and delicious food. Last night, we tasted the excitement and freshness of new fruits. We feel the sweetness of being in community together. And, on Rosh Hashana we aspire to do some hard work - to do teshuva and to daven to be inscribed in the Book of Life. This is not easy work. Each year, we struggle anew with how to accomplish these big and difficult tasks. There are many wonderful tools to be successful - the tefillot in our machzor, the sound of the shofar, the power of gathering together. I would like to offer another tool - one inspired by an odd group of three very different women we encounter on Rosh Hashana: Hagar, Hannah, and Eim Sisera, the mother of Sisera, the Canaanite general, who was just killed by Yael. They all share one thing in common, like perhaps some of us here will today. Today, they all cry in shul, heard through our liturgy. We witness Hagar and Hannah cry in Torah and Haftorah reading, and we hear the metaphorical wails of Eim Sisera in the sounds of the Shofar.

In our Torah reading this morning Avraham and Sara send away Hagar and her son, Yishmael. Alone and away from home, she is wandering in the desert with Yishmael, when she runs out of water. She bursts into tears at the thought of him dying of thirst. In the haftorah Hannah desperately yearns for a son. When her family goes to Shilo, she goes to daven, in her מָרַת נֶפֶשׁ, her distress, to ask God for a child, weeping all the while. Eim Sisera, the book of Shoftim tells us, is sitting, waiting for her son, the Cannanite general to arrive home from war. When she realizes her son has been defeated and killed, she lets out a wail.

Three different people, with different challenges, all respond by crying. In today's society we often are embarrassed by our tears. We put on our sunglasses, take a moment outside the room, clear our throat. We might say we have allergies. I have heard people jokingly ask "who is cutting onions in here" to make light of their tears. But the tears in these three stories are important and worth mentioning in the narrative. And not just once, but three times this morning. Anytime is repeated three times, we understand contains wisdom. So much so that we identify with and learn from Hagar and Sisera's mother, two women who generally fall outside of our internal communal narrative. There must be something about crying that helps each one of them navigate their challenge. I would like to suggest that the important factor is that tears are a sign of vulnerability.

Researcher Brene Brown, studies emotions of shame, fear and vulnerability. We see many of these emotions in our stories. All three characters are vulnerable - exposed to possible physical or emotional harm - exposed to the elements of the desert, to feeling disconnected, to feeling alone and feeling grief. These are feelings and emotions we all grapple with - Fear, inadequacy and grief. Danger, disconnection and aloneness.

We see vulnerability expressed through the tears in each story. Hagar's tears are tears of fear - fear of dying in the desert, of having to watch her child suffer, of being alone and without any support. Hannah's tears are tears of sadness, of feeling inadequate because she can't have children. Eim Sisera, wails. The wails of a mother who has heard her son will never return home to her again. Tears of grief, tears of loss. These are tears of despair that the Rabbis imagine sound like the broken notes

121

of the shevarim. We sound 100 blasts of the shofar, and we hear the 100 wails of Eim Sisera.

Each woman's tears are the expression of the choice to be vulnerable. Imagine if Hagar had allowed her fear to overwhelm her and she chose to kill her son before he died of thirst. If Hannah had become bitter and spiteful in her feelings of shame and inadequacy, if Eim Sisra had taken a sword to kill out of vengeance. How often do we, by hiding our vulnerability, make choices that serve to make us more fearful, more alone, more disconnected?

Brown explains when we can use vulnerability productively. When we don't let shame or fear deter us, we can feel connection. Through their tears, Hagar and Hannah seek connection and initiate an interaction with God. Perhaps Hagar does not intentionally start to pray, but her tears and the tears of her child seem to be interpreted as prayer or reaching out for connection to God. And sure enough, God responds with immediate help and a promise for Yishmael's future. Hannah goes to Shilo searching for a connection. God hears Hannah's tefillah, both in words and tears, and grants her a son, Shmuel. Although we don't know very much about Eim Sisera, we know that we use her cries through the sounds of the shofar to wake up our souls to search for connection.

It seems then that tears are not something to be ashamed of, or embarrassed by, but they are a sign that through our vulnerability we can find connection with God. Rabbi Elazar, in Massechet Brachot tells us that since the beit hamikdash was destroyed the gates of prayer - שַׁעֲרֵי תְפִילָה - are now locked. However, the gates of tears - שַׁעֲרֵי דִמְעָה - are never locked. Rabbi Elazar is reassuring us our tears, our vulnerability, will always connect us with God. We recite this idea in Neilah at the end of Yom Kippur, after all of the intense davening and Avodat

HaLev heart work we will do over the next ten days. We acknowledge in our tefillah, that the most meaningful moments came from a place of vulnerability, of tears. But we can't wait until Neilah. Our job over the next ten days, and throughout the year, is to find the שַׁעֲרֵי דִמְעָה - the gates of tears, the gates of vulnerability. If we rely only on the words in our machzor, we will get to the wrong gate. Just reciting tefillot brings us to a locked gate. We must find the gate that is open, we must use our vulnerability to find the שַׁעֲרֵי דִמְעָה.

What makes us vulnerable? We are vulnerable when we feel inadequate. We are vulnerable when we let ourselves be seen in our imperfections. We are vulnerable when we invest in a relationship - with God, with ourselves, our friends and community - that we know might not work out the way we wanted it to. Vulnerability is the letting go. Letting go of control. Letting go of shame. Letting go of fear. This is the path to feel connection, to allow ourselves to be seen. Really seen.

That means taking an honest accounting of ourselves and allowing that authentic self to be seen. Just this past week, I encountered an intense vulnerability and was tempted to avoid it. My daughter Ariella, like many kids, loves to document our lives and takes hours of videos on my phone, capturing snapshots of our daily life. I was watching them to determine which to delete, to free space on my phone. As you can imagine, mornings can be difficult in a busy house with four children who need to get out the door by 7:45 am. There are the particularly challenging moments - maybe they take place in your house too - spilled breakfast, forgotten lunches, missing socks. At first, I cringed when I heard how I sounded at these moments. There were more moments than I would like to admit where I raised my voice, spoke more sharply than I remember and certainly more than I intended. When I talk about my parenting strategies and skills, this is not how I think of myself. This is not the parent I aspire to be. I felt ashamed, vulnerable in front of myself and almost deleted them all without watching. But, after a moment's pause, I decided to sit with that vulnerability, to see myself - sometimes an irritable and impatient, overtired mom - because then I could use them to work on better parenting. I stepped back for a moment and thought - we all have moments where we are grateful, we are not being recorded. What would it look like to have to watch those moments today? Moments recorded throughout the year, video stored in the divine cloud. We all have moments where our reality, our response, does not match the aspirational pictures we hold of ourselves. How quick would we be to delete these moments? But by having the courage to review them, to sit with them, in vulnerability, we make room for growth, room for change.

Tefilla - truly standing before God, and teshuva - taking an honest accounting of one's actions and striving to correct them - are not easy tasks because they ask us to draw on this vulnerability - to let ourselves be seen, in our imperfection, to confront the places we want to make change. They are what Rav Yosef Baer Soloveitchik calls Avodat HaLev - heart work. With most mitzvot the act of doing the mitzva, the peulah, is equivalent to the fulfillment of the mitzvah, the kiyum hamitzvah. For example, to fulfill the mitzvah of sitting in your sukkah later this month, (the kiyum) you will sit in the sukkah (the peulah). However, there are a special mitzvot that require an emotional connection, an "avodat halev." On Sukkot, we are commanded "v'samachata bchagecha" - we must be happy on yom tov. There is not a clear path to the kiyum of this mitzvah. We eat special meals, sing songs and wear nice clothes, which can help us be happy, but they are not, themselves, the kiyum of the mitzvah to *feel* happy. In avodat halev mitzvot, the mitzvah often is defined by an action that is not guaranteed to produce the kiyum. There is a lot more effort and emotional work necessary in these mitzvot.

Brene Brown has a word for people who are successful at heart work - emotional and intentional work - the Whole Hearted. These are the people who embrace vulnerability and realize the opportunity vulnerability gives us to form connections. To form a connection with God we should be honest, open and real - with ourselves and with God. If, as we offer heartfelt prayers, that leads us to tears we don't have to hide them. Tears are just one, physical manifestation of vulnerability, but they are not the only one. All forms of vulnerability shows the true desire for connection. It shows our WholeHearted-ness, the Heart Work we did to get to that point. So perhaps the Shaarei Dima can be understood as the gates of vulnerability. When we can be vulnerable with God, the gates are never locked. Tears are one way to unlock them but all forms of wholehearted-ness - opening ourselves to vulnerability to form stronger connections - can open the gates of Shaarei Dima.

Tears are one peulah to fulfill the mitzvot of connecting to God through tefillah and doing Teshuva. No one peulah will guarantee this kiyum. For some tears do not resonate as a path to this mitzvah. For others, they yearn for tears but they feel out of reach. There is no right way to express vulnerability in search of connection. It is enough to do the emotional work. To be honest, to be grateful, to love with our whole hearts, to believe we are enough. Vulnerability could be being really honest with yourself as you take stock of the past year, watching some of the less ideal video footage in your mind. It could be leaning into your emotions and identifying them - fear, joy, disappointment, love - as you daven instead of brushing them aside to focus on the words in front of you. This is hard work, and we don't always know if we are doing it right. But if we open ourselves up - with honesty and candor, if we believe that through vulnerability comes connection, we can reach a place of stronger relationship with God. We, each of us, are worthy of divine connection and communal belonging.

One night, several years ago during Kabbalat Shabbat, I experienced a holy moment during davening. It was time for mourners kaddish and there was one young woman saying kaddish alone in the shul. She had lost her father a few short months ago. When she began the kaddish her voice wavered and in the middle of kaddish she began to cry. At that moment, the community stayed quiet. No one coughed or looked around or tried to rush her, we all just stood with her in her pain. In her vulnerable and real tears of loss. After a few moments the woman sitting next to her took her hand and, when the young woman began the kaddish they recited it together. I felt a transformation in the room. The room was charged with more intensity, more emotion for the rest of davening. When we, as a community, stood with her - stood as witness and made space for her vulnerability, her tears unlocked the gates - the shaarei dima for all of us in the room. As we enter into musaf, let us work together to open the gates. Some people in this room may be moved to tears. For some of us the tears will stain the pages of our machzor, for others they will remain in our eyes. For some of us, the tears remain in our hearts. All of these tears - physical and spiritual - are real. Some are the tears of connection with God, of showing God our true selves. Some are tears of sadness - over not receiving what we want in life, not feeling we are where we want to be. Some are tears of grief - who have we lost this year? What have we lost? All are tears of vulnerability. Of letting us be seen, in community, as imperfect, as real. These are the tears we strive for - the kiyum of the mitzvah to be close to God.

As a community we all stand together as one, allowing ourselves to feel vulnerability - through tears or in other, less visible ways. Supporting one another to feel those holy moments. Let us focus our intention and follow in the tears of Hagar. Of Eim Sisera. Of Hannah. To know that if we do, the gates of connection with Hashem are always open.

Standing Alone in Shiloh,
But Not Anymore
Hadassah Klein (Wendl)

Shiloh is where the Mishkan was established that had accompanied the Jewish people throughout their time in the desert. This place symbolizes another step in the transition from the Jewish people wandering in the desert to having a constant point of connection with God through the Temple in Jerusalem. Shiloh is also the place where Hannah, in I Shmuel, prayed for a child. We read about her and about Shiloh on Rosh Hashana as a haftara to the story of Sarah conceiving Yitzchak. Just like Sarah learnt that she would conceive a son on Rosh Hashana, Hannah's prayers for a child were heard in Shiloh on that very day.

Recently, I was reading Sarah Schenirer's Collected Writings (1935) which Naomi Seidman translated into English in 2019. In those, she discusses the impact of Hannah's prayer and what women can take from it nowadays. Sarah Schenirer was a trailblazing figure in interwar Jewish society who almost singlehandedly established the Bais Yaakov system, a network of hundreds of schools, camps and teacher training seminaries for Orthodox Jewish women in interwar Central Europe. Today, there are Bais Yaakov schools across the Jewish world, educating a wide range of Jewish girls from Modern Yeshivish to Chasidic backgrounds. All this started as supplementary afternoon classes in Sarah Schenirer's two-room apartment with 25 students in Krakow in 1917. Hannah's prayer established something new that would be impactful for her and her students.

Sarah Schenirer's Collected Writings (1935) include her previous articles as well as other writings on Jewish thought, the Bais Yaakov movement and Jewish education. In her article on Rosh Hashana, she links Hannah's prayer in Shiloh to the history of that place and the impact it had on the world of prayer. But Schenirer goes further than that, drawing parallels between Hannah standing alone in front of God in Shiloh and the situation of Jewish women's education in interwar Poland. In the book of Joshua, we learn that the whole community would assemble at Shiloh (Josh 18, Josh 22). This is where the Ohel Moed was set up and the Jewish people came to bring sacrifices and offerings. Within a few decades, though, Shiloh gradually lost its importance, Sarah Schenirer notes. Fewer and fewer people would come to the Mishkan to bring sacrifices. She remarks that the first chapter of Shmuel, which zooms in on that narrative, does not indicate the presence of anyone else around the Mishkan except for her and Eli, the High Priest. Hannah prayed there on her own.

Hannah's individual, lone prayer, which made Eli think she was drunk, had an immense impact on Jewish history and prayer. Ideally, Shiloh should be a place for the whole Jewish community to connect to God, but in the book of Shmuel it is just lonely Hannah, on her own, who goes there to do so. Her prayers for a child were heard. Months later she gave birth to Shmuel, who would bring about Israel's monarchy. It is from Hannah's way of praying that Chazal in bT Berachot 30b-31b also learn the principles of prayer. Through her words and actions, she laid the path for a whole new notion of community: the prayer community. Her achievement did not come without difficulties: Mocked by her co-wives and misunderstood by both her husband Elkana and Eli, the high priest, her steadfast devotion paved the way for the next step in Jewish history and for a new way of connecting to God outside a fixed place like Shiloh. This new community shares not a place, but words.

Like Hannah, Sarah Schenirer experienced in her own life that community can come from loneliness, from the feeling of being left out. Year after year, the male members of her Chassidic community would make their way to their rebbe for the Yamim Noraim. This tradition left women back home, without much opportunity to meaningfully connect to Rosh Hashana, Yom Kippur and Sukkot through communal prayer. Women's marginal role in Jewish life and learning motivated Sarah Schenirer to create a space for young Jewish women and girls. She wanted to enable them to come together, become invigorated by Jewish tradition and be passionate about Jewish life. Starting with afternoon classes for two dozen of students, her network of Bais Yaakov schools and camps soon spanned across Central Europe. It continued to grow after WWII in Jewish communities across the world.

Sarah Schenirer, after describing Hannah's impact on Jewish history and prayer, praises her for her accomplishments and encourages her Bais Yaakov students to emulate Hannah: Follow your desire to connect to God, study Torah and turn what you learn into reality:

> "First, learn! Learn the holy Torah, immerse yourselves in the words of our prophets. Contemplate the wisdom of our sages, learn the rules and the prayers, familiarize yourselves with the history of your people. Learn, Jewish daughters, learn, so that the Jewish spirit will awaken within you and inspire you to become a Hannah."

She further motivates readers to live what they learn and to continue building a community of Jewish women who pray, study and grow together.

In the interwar period, Sara Schenirer saw that Jewish society was at a transitional period. New forms of community and women's expression were needed, and Hannah's story could serve as a role model for these times. Sarah Schenirer urges us to see Hannah's prayer in Shiloh as a potential for transition and transformation. Prayer is meaningful, even when it feels like we are alone. It can serve as a cornerstone for the building of a community that honours and enables women to find their place in Judaism. When we read about Hannah this year, think about the impact she had on our world of prayer. Think about other Jewish women who created spaces for their own needs, wishes and interests and those of fellow women. How can we create new spaces for us today – and use those that exist already – that can link us back to Hannah's and Sara Schenirer's mission and impact?

Source:

Naomi Seidman, Sarah Schenirer and the Bais Yaakov Movement. A Revolution in the Name of Tradition (Liverpool: Liverpool University Press, 2019), 295.

Finding Inspiration in the Torah and Haftara Readings of Rosh Hashana

Sharona Margolin Halickman

When comparing the Torah and Haftorah readings of the first day of Rosh Hashana, a common theme jumps out at us. The theme is women desperately wanting a child and eventually being granted that child. The Torah reading deals with the story of Sarah and the eventual birth of Yitzchak. The Haftarah deals with the story of Channa and the eventual birth of Shmuel.

What do these readings have to do with Rosh Hashana? The Gemara in Brachot 29a states: On Rosh Hashana Sarah, Rachel and Channa were remembered (*nifkedu*). Each of these women became pregnant on Rosh Hashana.

This follows the theme of the *Zichronot* in the Rosh Hashana service. Just as God remembered Sarah, Rachel and Channa, we hope that due to their merits, God will remember us and grant us our requests.

Another reason why Channa's account is read on Rosh Hashana is because it shows the power of prayer. In Shmuel I 1:12 it says, "Now Channa spoke in her heart, only her lips moved, but her voice was not heard." In the Gemara in Brachot 31a Rav Hamnuna states that we can learn many laws of prayer from Channa. The fact that Channa had intense *kavana* (focus) during prayer teaches us that we too must have *kavana*. The fact that only her lips moved shows that we must pronounce each and every word with our lips. The fact that her voice was not heard shows that we can pray quietly and must not scream out. Channa actually set the precedent of how we pray today.

Yalkut Shimoni adds that the structure of the Shemoneh Esrei as we know it today is based on Channa's thanksgiving prayer. This teaches us the power of prayer and specifically the power of women's prayers on Roah Hashana as well as on a daily basis.

We learn from Channah that prayer can make an impact on our lives. We have the opportunity to try to emulate Channa's *kavana* during the High Holidays as well as throughout the year.

Let us hope and pray that our requests for the New Year will be granted.

HOPE in Our Time:
Second Day Rosh Hashana 2020
Nechama Liss-Levinson, Ph.D.

When my oldest sister was born, my parents named her Yehudit Chana. In English, Jacquelyn Harriet. They had considered naming her Jacquelyn Hope, but since our last name was Liss, she would have been Jackie HopeLESS.

And the idea of forever being HopeLESS was unthinkable.

This has been a year of despair and hopelessness for many. And so, This Rosh Hashana, amidst a global pandemic, climate change, and the continuing plagues of racism and anti-Semitism, THIS YEAR, we need to talk about HOPE.

In speaking about HOPE, I do not mean "I hope our team wins" or "I hope the weather will be nice tomorrow."

Rather, Hope is the torch we hold in times of darkness to help us see the path ahead. Hope is not a guarantee that everything will turn out the way we want. But hope gives us the strength keep going forward during uncertain and turbulent times. HOPE is often confused with optimism. Optimism is the belief that things will generally get better. Hope is the belief that WE can make things better. HOPE is a VERB.

Optimism sees the glass as half full.

Hope searches for a way to fill the glass.

The Hebrew word for HOPE is TIKVAH. It is found in the book of Joshua (Chapter 2). Two Jewish spies, sent to check out the land of Israel, find safety at the home of a prostitute with a golden heart, named Rachav. As the spies are leaving, Rachav wants assurance that her home will be a safe haven when the Jews return. The men choose a line of scarlet thread hung from her window as the sign. The line of thread is, "Chut Shani Tikva", tikva," coming from the Hebrew root of Kav, a straight line. This line of thread becomes her source of hope.

In these times, many of us feel like we are just holding on by a thread.

To go forward, we need hope. Hope for ourselves and hope we bring to others. Hope is a uniquely human quality. And according to Rabbi Jonathan Sacks, an essential Jewish quality.

To be a Jew, says Sacks, "is to be an agent of HOPE in a world threatened by despair."

HOPE moves us from what IS today to what COULD be tomorrow. HOPE acknowledges the obstacles that exist in getting from here to there.

But Hope does not deny reality and the obstacles we face. Instead, HOPE DEFIES reality.

The story of the founding of the state of Israel is just such a story.

Israel's National Anthem, HA TIKVA, meaning The Hope, was written in 1878 by the Polish poet, Naftali Herz Imber. The British banned the singing of this song briefly in 1919, because it inspired civic unrest. While preparing for today, I heard an extraordinary recording of a group of Survivors of Bergen Belsen, singing HaTikvah, 5 days after liberation, in April 1945. The words, "LO Avda Tikvataynu" We have NOT LOST our hope, are verbal acts of resistance to the Nazis, but also to

Ezekial's words, "Avda Tikvataynu!," "Our hope IS LOST".
(Chapter 37, v 11)

The sociologist Peter Berger calls hope:

> "… a signal of transcendence, a belief in something more than just ourselves, be it God, community or a force beyond us we don't understand. Through hope we can overcome the difficulties of any given here and now."

British Rabbi Hugo Gryn told a story of himself as a child in Auschwitz. As Hanukkah approached, Hugo's father asked him to create some wicks for candles from the threads of his uniform (perhaps a later incarnation of Rachav's scarlet thread.) His father had carefully saved their tiny ration of margarine, and using the wicks, they attempted to light Chanukah candles. Little Hugo was angry that his father was wasting the precious margarine. His father wisely responded,

> "You know, dear child, we can go three days without water and even longer without food, but a person cannot live even one day without hope."

So what does hope look like today?

Hope is planting a garden during a plague.
Hope is bringing flowers from that garden to the Shabbat table of someone who lives alone.
Hope is amazing quarantine cooking.
Hope is delivering those amazing casseroles to a food pantry to feed the hungry.
Hope is teaching Torah Trop to a child for next year's Bar or Bat Mitzvah.
Hope is practicing English conversation with a refugee who now calls America home.
Hope is VOTING.

Hope is getting married during a pandemic.

So, HOW do we get to HOPE?

Hope, like many traits we desire, requires effort on our part. Like a muscle we wish to develop, we need a workout routine to cultivate hope.

Luckily for us, the Rosh Hashana liturgy offers a plan to grow HOPE for ourselves and to bring as a gift to others. In a few minutes time, after the blowing of the shofar to SHAKE US AWAKE, comes the UnTaneh Tokef Prayer,

> On Rosh Hashana it is written and on Yom Kippur it is sealed/ Who Shall Live and who shall Die....

And although this prayer expresses the tragic dimensions of human existence, it also offers us three pathways forward.

> *UTShuvah, UTefilah UTzedakah, Maavirin Et Roa HaGzera.*
> And Repentance, and Prayer, and Justice transform
> the harshness of the decree.

These three words, Repentance, Prayer and Justice, are nouns. It is our responsibility to make them VERBS. That is the alchemy of turning despair into hope.

Let's start with: **Teshuva,** Repentance

The Mitzvah of teshuva **begins** with self-assessment of our past behaviors, but it is only **fulfilled** when we behave **differently** in the future. Teshuva reminds that we have the POWER to Change OURSELVES.

Dr. Jerome Groopman, in his book, The Anatomy of Hope, writes:

> "Hope can only flourish when you believe that what you do CAN make a difference, that your actions CAN bring a future different from your present…"

As a therapist, during these last six months, I heard so many people speak about their growing awareness of what truly mattered. Family, Friends, Faith, Nature. And in dozens of small acts of teshuva, they often changed their behaviors to align with who they hoped to be.

Tefila

Prayer, the second strategy for attaining hope, can be both comforting and elusive.

My mother-in-law, Sylvia Levinson, felt like she had a DIRECT LINE, that KAV, to God. She would speak to God as an intimate. But not everyone is blessed with that direct line. For some of us, the cell tower is down, and our reception is sketchy. We are left grasping for that thread.

We may want to believe, as Peter Berger wrote, that the universe is not "deaf to our prayers…… indifferent to our existence." But it's not always easy.

For some people, hope in prayer involves pleading for a specific outcome. But for others, the hope we seek in prayer is that we will get through this time, that we gain strength to face our pain, that God watch over us, that our loved ones feel uplifted, that our lives be filled with blessings and that we bring blessing to others.

My mother loved the Refuah Shelamah prayer. She prayed for strength & renewal for those who were ill and wisdom for their doctors. She also prayed with her presence, through long conversations on the phone and with the foods she brought to those who needed comfort. Her prayers brought healing of spirit, her prayers brought hope.

But for some, hope still feels elusive. My dear friend, Rabbi Sharyn Perlman suggests that these individuals can begin by hoping for hope.

In the Shemoneh Esrah, Silent Amidah, of the Days of Awe, we pray:

> Tayn Tikvah l'Dorshecha.
> Give hope to those who seek you.

It is also a prayer for many today. Please God, Give hope to those who NEED HOPE.

Tzedakah, Justice or Charity, is a bubbling wellspring of hope.

Judaism teaches that we are God's partner in healing this broken world. And the broken shards are everywhere.

We live amidst rising hunger, homelessness, devouring wildfires, and systemic racism. It is our obligation, as Jews, to use our gifts, our time, our talents, our finances to pursue justice, to do tzekakah, to bring forth hope.

We may not see the fulfillment of our efforts. But it is our task to begin. To quote Anne Frank, "How wonderful it is that nobody need wait a single moment before starting to improve the world."

I'm going to end the Dvar with a story I think Anne Frank would have enjoyed.

> The British centenarian, Capt. Tom Moore decided to raise funds for covid relief by walking 100 laps for his 100th birthday, all in his backyard. Captain Tom became a media sensation, as people watched him walk a few laps each day, assisted only by his trusty walker.
>
> As part of the fundraising effort, he recorded a song with the National Health Services Choir.
>
> The song, which immediately reached Number ONE in the English Hit Parade, was the 1945 Rogers and Hammerstein favorite, "You'll Never Walk Alone."

The peak moment in the song is "Walk on, walk on, with **HOPE** in your heart and you'll **never walk alone**."

When so many of us are feeling alone, what do these words really mean?

I think that having hope in your heart means that you believe that your life has meaning. It means you believe in something BEYOND yourself, whether that be God, your family, your community, the souls of loved ones or your ideals and dreams. They will be by your side and within you, bringing you HOPE and at other times, YOU providing hope for THEM, and therefore, you will, never be alone.

By the way, Capt. Tom raised 32 million pounds or over $42 million dollars for covid relief.

In 2003, Rabbis Lisa Gelber and Cindy Enger created a Haggadah for women who had experienced domestic violence. They began the Seder with the words: "Nazmin et

Mekor Hatikvah L'Kirbeinu," Let us invite the SOURCE of HOPE into our Midst.

As we continue our prayers today,
Let us invite the SOURCE OF HOPE into our midst.
Let the piercing sounds of shofar enter your soul.
Let our hopes rise.
Search deep inside, reach for the strengths that God has given you.
Let our hopes rise.
Shape these strengths into actions to lift yourself and to lift others up.
Let our hopes rise.
Reach out to the community that embraces you.
Rise UP.
Together, we can kindle infinite sparks of HOPE to illuminate the world.

Shanah Tovah.

Women and Shofar:
Evolution of a Communal Practice
Rabbanit Gloria Nusbacher

Perhaps more than any other mitzva (with the possible exception of *Megillat Esther*), most synagogues today go out of their way to enable women to hear shofar – through extra blowings at shul and sending people to blow for homebound women. The development of this practice provides an instructive example of how women's embracing of a ritual can influence community practices.

Talmudic Background

The Mishnah states that "Every positive time-bound mitzva (*kol mitzvat aseh she-hazman grama*) — men are obligated and women are exempt (*patur*) (Kiddushin 1:7). The Gemara on this mishnah elaborates on this point: The Sages taught: What is a positive time-bound mitzva? Sukka, lulav, shofar, tzitzit and tefillin (Kiddushin 33b-34a). While the Gemara challenges the mishnah by pointing out some of the exceptions to the rule, it ends up affirming the general principle that women are exempt from positive time-bound *mitzvot*.

When discussing the mitzva of shofar, the Gemara goes beyond stating that women are exempt, and considers whether they are even permitted to do this mitzva. The discussion begins with a statement in the Mishnah that "one does not prevent children from blowing [the shofar]" (Rosh Hashana 4:8). The Gemara reads this mishnah to imply that we <u>do</u> stop women from blowing the shofar — since both women and children are exempt from positive time-bound *mitzvot* such as shofar, if the mishnah says we don't stop children from blowing shofar, this must mean that we do stop women from blowing. (Rosh Hashana 33a).

The Gemara then challenges this implication:

> Isn't it taught in a *baraita* that we don't prevent either women or children from blowing the shofar on yom tov? Abaye said this is not difficult — [the mishna] is in accordance with the opinion of Rabbi Yehuda, and [the *baraita*] is in accordance with the opinion of Rabbi Yosi and Rabbi Shimon. (Rosh Hashana 33a)

We see that there are two views reflected in the Gemara as to whether women are permitted to perform the mitzva of blowing shofar — Rabbi Yehuda in the mishnah says they are not, while Rabbi Yosi and Rabbi Shimon in the *baraita* say that they are permitted.

A possible basis for Rabbi Yosi's opinion is described in Gemara Hagiga. The topic under discussion is whether women are permitted to perform the ritual act of *smikha* (pressing their hands on the animal) before it is slaughtered as a *korban* (sacrifice):

Men do *smikha* but women do not. Rabbi Yosi and Rabbi Yishmael say for women *smikha* is permitted but optional (*reshut*). Rabbi Yosi said: Abba Elazar told me that one time we had a calf for a *korban shlamim* (a peace-offering sacrifice) and we brought it to the *ezrat nashim* (the Women's Courtyard in the Temple) and the women did *smikha* on it — not because women are obligated to do *smikha*, but in order to provide *nachat ruach* (spiritual satisfaction) for the women.

Under this approach, women who perform a ritual act from which they are exempt are not really doing a mitzva — they are just given permission to do something that would otherwise

143

be forbidden, in order to provide them with spiritual satisfaction.

Theoretical Approaches of the Rishonim

The conflicting positions in the Gemara lead the *Rishonim* (medieval commentaries) to take a variety of positions regarding women and shofar. Rashi, based on Rosh Hashana 33a, holds that women are prohibited from blowing shofar:

We prevent women [from blowing] because they are completely exempt, since it [shofar] is a positive time-bound mitzva; and if they would blow, it would be a violation of *baal tosif* (the prohibition on adding to the *mitzvot* of the Torah) (Rashi, Rosh Hashana 33a, s.v. *ha nashim m'akhvin*)

Rambam, apparently based on Hagiga 16b, holds that, as is the case with all positive time-bound *mitzvot*, women are permitted to blow shofar, but since they are not performing a mitzva, they do so without a *bracha*:

> Women or slaves who want to wear tzitzit may do so without a *bracha*. And this is so for all positive *mitzvot* from which women are exempt — if they want to do them without a *bracha*, no objection is raised. (Rambam, Mishneh Torah, *Hilkhot Tzitzit* 3:9)

Tosafot, commenting on Rosh Hashana 33a, expressly adopts the position of Rabbi Yosi in the *baraita*. However, even though Rabbi Yosi holds that women may perform a ritual act solely in order to derive spiritual satisfaction, and thus does not consider it performance of a mitzva, Tosafot holds that women are permitted to recite a *bracha* on their action:

Rabbenu Tam (12th century France) said even though the unattributed position in the Mishnah [referred to in Rosh

144

Hashana 33a] is that of Rabbi Yehuda, the *halakha* follows the position of Rabbi Yosi [who said that women are permitted to blow shofar].... And they are permitted to make a *bracha* on a positive time-bound mitzva even though they are exempt from that mitzva. (Tosafot, Rosh Hashana 33a, s.v. *ha Rabbi Yehuda, ha Rabbi Yosi*)

The most expansive position of the *Rishonim* is that of Rashba (13th century Spain). Commenting on Rosh Hashana 33a, he states:

Women are permitted to make a *bracha* on all positive time-bound *mitzvot*, even though they are only optional for women (*reshut*). In any case, they are engaging in a mitzva and it is an obligation. Although God did not obligate them to do like men, if they want to do it we call it *ve-tzivanu* ("and He commanded us").

Rashba's position appears to be derived from Kiddushin 31a, which provides that "Greater is one who is commanded to do a mitzva than who is not commanded and does it." The assumption behind this statement is that an act that is designated a mitzva is still a mitzva, even if done by someone who is not commanded to do it. The quoted statement is made in connection with a story about a non-Jew who fulfilled the mitzva of *kibud av* (honoring one's father). The Sages wanted to buy precious stones from this non-Jew at a price which would have earned him a large profit. But in order to make the sale he would have had to get the gems from the room where his father was sleeping. Rather than risk waking his father, he refused to make the sale. God rewarded him by having a *para aduma* (red heifer) born to his flock, which he sold to the Sages for an even greater profit. Rabbi Chanina cited this incident as proof that God rewards those who do a mitzva, even if they are not obligated to do that mitzva, and then makes the statement quoted above.

Later poskim articulated an additional rationale for allowing women to blow shofar — that they have taken this obligation upon themselves. For example, Maharil (14th-15th century Germany) states:

Indeed, women are exempt [from shofar] as it is a positive time-bound commandment. But they bring themselves into the obligation. Since they obligate themselves, they need to hurry to finish their needs — jewelry or cooking — to be free to come to shul and be there to hear the shofar, and they should not force the congregation to wait for them. ...

> In Austria the women would cook on Erev Rosh Hashana for Rosh Hashana and be free to be in shul on Rosh Hashana, and when they left shul they would heat up the food. And everyone would try to be in shul, women and girls, to hear the prayers and the *tekiyot* (shofar blasts) from beginning to end. And this is the practice now. (Maharil, *Hilkhot Shofar*)

Maharil is describing an already-established practice of women coming to shul specifically on Rosh Hashana. His statement that women need to get there on time so that they don't force the congregation to wait for them indicates that women hearing the shofar was seen as important enough that the community would wait for them if they were late.

Practical Implications

Blowing by women. Under all of the theoretical approaches except that of Rashi, a woman is permitted to blow shofar for herself. The only difference among the various approaches is whether she can make the *bracha* before blowing. The Shulchan Aruch, following Rambam, holds that women cannot make the *bracha* because they are exempt from the mitzva. The Rema, reflecting the Ashkenazic practice, holds that women do make *brachot* on positive time-bound *mitzvot* even though they are exempt.

Similarly, a woman is permitted to blow shofar for other women, since all have the same level of obligation. The limiting factor here is that, at least until fairly recently, most women did not have the knowledge and skills to enable them to blow shofar, so their theoretical ability had little practical effect.

There is a further limitation with respect to women blowing for men. As a general principle, a person who is not obligated to perform a mitzva cannot discharge the obligation of members of the community who are obligated in that mitzva. (Mishnah Rosh Hashana 3:8). Men are obligated in shofar on a Torah level, and women are *patur* (exempt) — not obligated in this mitzva, even on a rabbinic level. Therefore, even under the most expansive view, that they have taken the mitzva upon themselves, women have a lesser level of obligation than that of men, so blowing by women cannot fulfill the obligation of men.

Blowing by Men for Women. The general rule is that a man can blow shofar for another man even if the first man has already fulfilled his obligation. This is based on the principle of *areivut (kol Yisrael arevim zeh la'zeh)* — all Israel are responsible for each other. How this principle applies to a man blowing shofar for a woman depends on the way the posek sees women's relationship to the mitzva of shofar.

Under the view that shofar is a mitzva for women even though they are exempt, a man may blow for a woman even if he has already fulfilled his obligation. In other words, a woman is treated no differently than a man in this regard. This view is expressed by the Rav'ya, one of the German Tosafot (12-13th century):

> The law is that one may blow [shofar] for them [women], for it is a skill and not a Torah-prohibited *melacha*. And a man may blow for them even if he has already fulfilled his obligation. And since there is a mitzva, for women may [blow] for themselves if they want, ... it is also permitted to carry a shofar for them in the public domain.... And even one who is not commanded also has a small part in the commandment. (Rav'ya - part II Rosh Hashana 534)

We see a more contemporary expression of this idea by Rav Moshe Feinstein. Rav Moshe starts from the premise that a person cannot carry a shofar on Yom Tov unless it's for the purpose of a mitzva. Then he says that just as carrying it for men is considered for purposes of a mitzva, so too is carrying it to enable women to do the mitzva:

> [E]ven for women it [carrying the shofar] is a great need (*tzorech gadol*), since they are fulfilling the mitzva and they get a reward (*s'char*). And who is to say that there is a need that allows the blowing only for one who has an obligation and is receiving reward as an obligated person, but not for one who has no obligation and is receiving reward as a non-obligated person? Even a mitzva done by someone who is not obligated is a great thing and its reward is eternal and better than all of life in this world. (Igrot Moshe, Orach Chayim 3:94)

There is an added degree of complexity if shofar is not seen as a mitzva for women. In that case, a man who has not yet satisfied his own obligation could blow for the woman and could recite the *bracha*—he is satisfying his own obligation, and her involvement is incidental. Similarly, a man who has already fulfilled his obligation could blow (with a *bracha*) for another <u>man</u> who has not heard shofar; a woman could listen, but her involvement would be seen as incidental.

The poskim are divided when it comes to whether a man who has already fulfilled his own obligation can blow just for a woman. The Rema holds that the man may blow for her, but should not make the *bracha*. (He appears to hold, however, that the woman may recite the *bracha* for herself.) (Orach Chayim 589:6)

Other poskim hold that a man who has already fulfilled his own obligation would not even be permitted to blow just for a woman. Poskim taking this approach have raised two types of objections. To some, this blowing would be a violation of Yom Tov (*Hagahot Maimoniot, Hilchot Shofar* 2:1), while to others it would not be an actual violation, but merely a weekday activity (*uvdah de-chol*) (See Ran on the Rif, Shabbat 2a). In either case, the rationale is that if hearing shofar is not a mitzva for women, blowing for them is no different than blowing a trumpet.

But even those poskim who followed this approach made a concerted effort to provide for men to be available to blow shofar for women who could not get to shul. For example, Ra'avan, an early German Tosafist, wrote as follows:

> [I]t seems that it would be prohibited for a man who is obligated in *mitzvot* to blow for them [women], unless he is blowing for a man who is obligated and they also happen to hear. And I wondered how earlier generations would blow for new mothers or for a sick woman. And it seems to me that this is what they would do: the *toke'a* [blower] would intend to fulfill his own obligation [when blowing for the woman] and this is how they permitted this, since he fulfills his own obligation with his blowing. But if he has already fulfilled his obligation, I wonder how he is allowed to blow

the shofar, unless I say that ... since one is allowed to blow shofar [on Rosh Hashana] when there is a need (*tzorech*), it is also permitted when there is no need. (Ra'avan, Rosh Hashana)

The Ra'avan's reasoning is based on the principle of *mi-toch*, which basically says if a *melacha* is permitted on Yom Tov for one purpose, that act is permitted for other Yom Tov-related purposes as well. Since a man who has already fulfilled his obligation is permitted to blow shofar for a man who has not yet heard shofar in order to enable the second man to fulfill his obligation, that same act of blowing the shofar would be permitted to be done for a woman, even though for her there is neither obligation nor mitzva.

Here we see an effort to have men wait to fulfill their own obligation until they were at the home of a woman who couldn't get to shul, so that the man could blow shofar for the woman. But where that was impossible, the Ra'avan interpreted the halacha to find a way to permit him to blow for her anyway.

Similarly, the Magen Avraham (17th century Poland) expresses a preference that a man who will blow shofar for a woman should avoid hearing the shofar blown in shul. However, if for some reason this is impossible, for example because he is the only shofar blower in his shul, "then he should intend not to fulfill his obligation through the blasts in synagogue, and then he can make the blessing for [women]." (Magen Avraham on Shulchan Aruch, Orach Chayim 589:6.) Here, too, the posek calls on the man to use "negative *kavana*," a form of legal fiction, to enable women to hear shofar with a *bracha*.

Conclusion

The Talmud was ambivalent regarding women's participation in the mitzva of shofar. They were either exempt from the mitzva, prohibited from performing it, or allowed to perform it for spiritual satisfaction but not as a mitzva. The *Rishonim* articulated a number of theoretical approaches to women's participation in the mitzva based on the statements in the Gemara they chose to prioritize. These ranged from a minority position that women were prohibited to blow shofar, to the position that they could blow without a *bracha*, to the position that blowing shofar was a mitzva for women albeit one they were not obligated in. some later poskim saw shofar as an obligation that women had taken upon themselves.

Most poskim concluded that women could blow shofar for themselves and for other women, with their primary disagreement over whether they could recite the *bracha*. But this halakhic conclusion had little practical effect since most women lacked the knowledge and skills to blow shofar.

While all poskim agreed that a man who had not yet satisfied his own obligation, or was satisfying the obligation of another man, could blow shofar for a woman, they disagreed in the case where the man had already fulfilled his own obligation and was blowing only for a woman. Poskim who saw women's participation in shofar as fulfillment of mitzva held that such a man could blow for a woman in the same way he could blow for a man. But even those poskim who held there was no obligation for women to hear shofar found ways to enable women who could not get to shul to hear shofar. Ideally, this was done by making available a man who had not yet satisfied his own obligation. But when this was impossible, they found halakhic theories and legal fictions to allow men to blow for the women anyway.

It is not clear why hearing shofar became such a popular ritual for women, but it is clear that as early as the 14th-15th century it was an established practice for women to come to shul particularly on Rosh Hashana to hear shofar. And it seems reasonable that because the mitzva of shofar was so eagerly embraced by women, communities and poskim found ways to further enable their participation in this mitzva.

Rabbanit Gloria Nusbacher *has* semikhah *from Yeshivat Maharat and currently serves as a community educator. Previously, she was a partner at one of the 100 largest U.S. law firms. She is a member of the* Jofa Journal *Editorial Board.*

Change We Can Believe In

Rabbanit Aliza Sperling
Ronda Angel Arking, Editor

(Previously published on Jofa.org)

The High Holiday period is punctuated with the theme of change. But how many times can we hear about change during the High Holidays without becoming cynical? For many of us, little has changed since last year. Many of the problems we face have not gone away—or may have even gotten worse. Our relationships, our communities, and the world around us have not appreciably changed for the better. Is it possible to break free of our stasis and change the problems that plague us? How can we make this Yom Kippur different, and truly grow and change over the course of the coming year?

A key to this question may lie in a biblical story that we all know so well we hardly give it a second thought: the story of Moshe and the burning bush. When Moshe stops to consider why the bush is burning but not consumed, God reveals the divine name Ehyeh, and announces that this force will redeem the people from slavery.

Rav Hirsch explains that the name *Ehyeh* expresses God's absolute freedom—and the name itself empowers humans:

> All other creatures are that which they have to be... [but God] alone can say..." I shall be that which I wish to be." This expresses the personal, absolute free nature of God... The future is completely unbound, completely dependent on [God's] free will. . .. [This name] breaks the chain of every other power, sets [Humanity] upright and free in the service of God.

The name *Ehyeh* symbolizes God's radical freedom: God is a force beyond nature, time, and human assumptions about the world. When God brings this liberating power into history, everything changes. A bush can defy nature and The name *Ehyeh* symbolizes God's radical freedom: God is a force beyond nature, time, and human assumptions about the world. When God brings this liberating power into history, everything changes. A bush can defy nature and burn without being consumed. A slave nation can free itself spectacularly from the most powerful nation on earth. Our world no longer must be constrained by the laws and expectations that we believe imprison us; there are possibilities and freedoms open to us if only we would free our minds to see them.

In our personal lives, as well, new possibilities emerge. Instead of believing that we are branded permanently by previous actions, we can transcend our misdeeds through teshuvah, repentance, and grow and change to become different people. We have the radical ability to free ourselves from who we are and transform into the people we want to be.

The importance—and difficulty—of freeing ourselves to change and live up to our potential is illustrated by the story of Rabbi Yochanan and Reish Lakish (BT Bava Metzia 84a):

יומא חד הוה קא סחי ר 'יוחנן בירדנא חזייה ריש לקיש ושוור לירדנא אבתריה
אמר ליה חילך לאורייתא אמר ליה שופרך לנשי א"ל אי הדרת בך יהיבנא לך
אחותי דשפירא מינאי קביל עליה בעי למיהדר לאתויי מאניה ולא מצי הדר
אקרייה ואתנייה ושווייה גברא רבא

One day R. Yochanan was bathing in the Jordan, when Reish Lakish saw him and leaped into the Jordan after him.

R. Yochanan said to him, "Your strength should be for the Torah!" "Your beauty," Reish Lakish replied, "should be for women." "If you will return to Torah,' said Rabbi Yochanan, "I will give you my sister [in marriage], who is more

beautiful than I.' Reish Lakish accepted this offer...
Subsequently, Rabbi Yochanan taught him Bible and
Mishnah, and made him into a great man.

The midrash starts off entertainingly as the handsome Rabbi
Yochanan and the well-known bandit Reish Lakish meet in the
Jordan River. Each man immediately sees in the other the
potential for his own line of work. Rabbi Yochanan tells Reish
Lakish to use his strength to become a Torah scholar. Reish
Lakish in turn tells Rabbi Yochanan that he should use his
good looks to attract women. Both men have the ability to see
the other (but not the sister) as they are at the moment, as well
as the potential of what they can become. Perhaps it is no
coincidence that they meet in the river, a symbol of movement
and flow. In a true act of strength, Reish Lakish agrees to
change his life and becomes a great Torah scholar.

The story then continues to describe a halakhic argument
between these two men, which occurs long after Reish Lakish's
days as a bandit. The two men are debating the point at which
weapons are completed and therefore susceptible to ritual
impurity. Rabbi Yochanan argues that a weapon is completed
when it is forged in fire. Reish Lakish argues that a weapon is
not considered complete until a later stage of the process:
when it is rinsed in water. While the surface argument centers
on weapons, in fact this halakhic argument goes to the heart of
their relationship. At what point is a person complete? Is the
way we are the way we will always be, or can we say that
people have real potential to continue to grow, develop, and
change?

Rabbi Yochanan responds to Reish Lakish's halakhic point
with a comment that references Reish Lakish's earlier life: "The
bandit knows his trade." Reish Lakish, who thought he had
put that life behind him, suddenly suspects that his hard work
to become a "great man" has not changed the way Rabbi

155

Yochanan perceives him. He questions whether Rabbi Yochanan's intervention in his life has benefited him.

After this exchange, Rabbi Yochanan and Reish Lakish's relationship shatters—as does each man individually. Rabbi Yochanan becomes depressed, and Reish Lakish falls sick and dies.

In order to comfort Rabbi Yochanan, the rabbis send Rabbi Elazar ben Pedat to become his study partner. Rabbi Elazar is the opposite of Reish Lakish: he supports everything Rabbi Yochanan says, instead of challenging him as a rival. Rabbi Yochanan, who thrives in a world of challenge and growth, is inconsolable when he realizes that the only person capable of helping him move forward is gone. Perhaps this stasis in the Beit Midrash also causes him to regret the static, inflexible, person he appears to be during and after his altercation with Reish Lakish. He cries out until he loses his mind and dies.

When Reish Lakish and Rabbi Yochanan first meet in the Jordan River, they are exuberantly alive, able to perceive the potential in each other. At the end of the story, though, they have caused each other's demise. Rabbi Yochanan initially challenged Reish Lakish to change and grow, and Reish Lakish became an exciting learning partner for him. But when Rabbi Yochanan is vulnerable – when he is seriously challenged in debate or when he feels that Reish Lakish does not appreciate him – he views Reish Lakish as a threat rather than a partner. Both men become frozen in their positions, unable to find a way forward. Their deaths are really only a reflection of the stasis from which they are unable to emerge.

The story of Rabbi Yochanan and Reish Lakish is a sobering counterpoint to the hopeful message at the burning bush. But we can learn from this cautionary tale important lessons on how to achieve the promise of freedom and potential that God presents to Moshe:

- **Pursue potential:** The story of Rabbi Yochanan and Reish Lakish shows the possibility of pushing ourselves to become someone new and to create a new trajectory in our lives. Reish Lakish changes his life in response to Rabbi Yochanan's intervention and becomes a great man. We, too, should embrace opportunities to grow and change.

- **See ourselves and others for who we are now:** Reish Lakish is cut to the quick when Rabbi Yochanan calls him a bandit and responds by questioning whether his transformation was worthwhile. Doubt and cynicism can destroy years of hard work. We need to give ourselves and others the freedom to change and grow. Furthermore, when we interact with others, we need to see the people they are now and resist the temptation to view them as they used to be.

- **Embrace challenges:** Rabbi Yochanan and Reish Lakish pushed each other in the Bet Midrash and in their personal lives. When they responded positively to the challenge, they became better people and Torah scholars. When they treated the challenges as threats, their relationship collapsed. Challenges, or challenging people, may not always seem like gifts, but they help us grow. We should surround ourselves with people who challenge us positively— and welcome their challenges as growth opportunities.

God's revelation at the burning bush presents us with a divine imperative: to transcend the limitations that we believe fetter us and to become truly free. We lose out when we ignore this idea and assume that the status quo is our only realistic option. Certainly, making the decision to deeply change course and pursue our true potential is scary; but as Rabbi Yochanan learns in the end, the alternative, leading a life without growth, is not worth living. This Yom Kippur, if we embrace the radical freedom that God has revealed to us, the change we can accomplish can truly be redemptive.

The Journey of Teshuvah

Rabba Dr. Lindsey Taylor-Guthartz, London

The metaphor of a journey is very useful for thinking about the period from Rosh Hashana to Yom Kippur. During the High Holidays we travel from a universal festival, the acknowledgement of God as creator and monarch of the universe at Rosh Hashana, and end up at the very individual, personal encounter with God that each of us faces on Yom Kippur. Our tradition furnishes us with many ways to make this journey more vivid and meaningful---the magnificent and elaborate *piyutim*, prayer-poems, that we sing; the triple themes of kingships, remembrances, and *shofarot* that we use in the Amidah of Rosh Hashana; the heartfelt community pleading of Avinu Malkenu, when we ask for protection and the fulfilment of our needs in the year ahead. And there are so many different meanings we can find in the shofar blasts---from its links to the Akedah, when God's mercy overcame God's judgement, to its connection to the end of time and the 'day of the Lord' when the shofar will summon the world to judgement.

But in spite of all these aids, we often find it difficult to make the journey of *teshuvah*, repentance. We all know we're meant to 'do' it, and we all recite the various prayers that express our collective desire to change our lives and be better people. But as well as expressing our aspirations as a community, this journey is one that each of us has to do on our own. And how do you do that? It's not very clear. Where do you start? What are you actually meant to do? How do you know you've done it properly? Often, I end up just thinking a bit about arguments with family members and feeling sorry in a general way (though also defensive), and then at the end of Yom Kippur, I feel deflated and let down, as though I haven't really achieved anything. Perhaps it's time to think about the process of doing *teshuvah,* and to explore ideas that might help us on the way. Of course, some people may already have a tried and trusted technique that they use every year, which is fantastic, but I suspect that I am not the only one who needs to think more about this process and how to manage it.

To embody this sense of trying to do something that is outside our comfort zones, I'm going to explore some ideas from hasidic literature---a field of which I know little, and which I don't always feel drawn to. One of the things that often bothers me about many hasidic stories is their presentation of super-sensitive and perfect hasidic rebbes, all of them ready to burst into tears over their (presumably) next to non-existent sins. What is left for us mortals to learn from these saintly people? They don't seem to live in our world of uncertainty and doubts. But what I *do* find attractive and useful in the world of hasidic literature is the unparalleled ability of so many hasidic masters to reimagine classical texts, especially ones from Tanakh, in completely new and startling ways---a sort of Zen approach to text that transforms it into something totally new. Today I want to discuss an idea of R Zusya (or Zusha) of (H)Anipol (1718–1800), who belonged to the third generation of hasidic sages. He was the brother of Rabbi Elimelekh of Lyzhansk, and they were both students of the Maggid of Mezhritz. But before I explore his ideas, I want to look at two stories about him that address both my hesitation about hasidic rebbes, and my admiration of their textual skills.

You may very well have heard the first story, which tells of Rabbi Zusya when he was on his deathbed. His students saw him weeping, and asked, 'Rebbe, why are you so sad? After all the good deeds you have done, like Moshe, like Avraham, you must be expecting a great reward in the next world!' But Rabbi Zusya continued to weep, and replied, 'When I reach the next world, God will not ask me why I was not more like Moshe, or more like Avraham; God will ask me why I wasn't more like

Zusya! And what will I say?' Here is a clear answer to my concern about many hasidic stories ---this one tells us that we *don't* have to emulate the stories of hasidic rebbes of old. We don't have to do *teshuvah* like anyone else, and perhaps there is no perfect way of doing it. What we do have to do is what we are each capable of, to find our own way, our own level, so that we know we have made some sort of progress in our own terms, even if we haven't gone all the way. Each person is different and will approach the process of doing *teshuvah* in a different way. We have to do our own personal job, whatever that is---and really, we are the only people qualified to decide what that personal journey of *teshuvah* should look like.

The second story about Rabbi Zusya is a classic one of hasidic reinterpretation, in this case of a text that doesn't look at all inspirational. It appears that Rabbi Zusya had asked to study Mishnah with another hasidic master, who began with the very first mishnah, in tractate *Berakhot*: *me'ematai korin et shema ba'aravit*? He translated it in the usual way - 'From when do we read the Shema in the evening?' This is the standard way of understanding the phrase, and from here the Mishnah goes on to discuss various suggestions for the precise time from which evening Shema can be read. Rabbi Zusya, however, reread it with a tiny revocalization---*me'emati korin et shema ba'aravit*--- which can be translated as 'Out of awe we read the Shema in the evening'. Rabbi Zusya isn't interested in the technical details of the timing of the evening Shema, but in the spiritual preparation and mood in which we recite it. This is that 'Zen' moment of hasidic interpretation at its most striking---from a basic question of the timing of a ritual, we are transported to the deepest level of why and how we should perform rituals, to our receptivity to the divine in all that we do.

With this in mind, I'll move to another teaching of Rabbi Zusya, in which we have a chance to reread texts in the context of *teshuvah*.

'Rabbi Zusya said: There are 5 verses that constitute the essence of Judaism, and their first letters form the word *teshuvah*:

1. תָּמִים תִּהְיֶה עִם ה״ אֱלֹקֶיךָ:

You must be *tamim* with the LORD your God. (Devarim 18: 13)

2. שִׁוִּיתִי ה״ לְנֶגְדִּי תָמִיד כִּי מִימִינִי בַּל־אֶמּוֹט;

I have placed the Lord always opposite me;
[He is at my right hand; I shall never be shaken.] (Tehilim 16: 8)

3. לֹא־תִקֹּם וְלֹא־תִטֹּר אֶת־בְּנֵי עַמֶּךָ וְאָהַבְתָּ לְרֵעֲךָ כָּמוֹךָ אֲנִי ה״:

[You shall not take vengeance or bear a grudge against your countrymen.] **Love your fellow person as yourself**: I am the LORD. (Vayikra 19: 18)

4. בְּכָל־דְּרָכֶיךָ דָעֵהוּ וְהוּא יְיַשֵּׁר אֹרְחֹתֶיךָ:

In all your ways know Him,
[And He will make your paths smooth]. (Mishlei 3: 6)

5. הִגִּיד לְךָ אָדָם מַה־טּוֹב וּמָה־ה״ דּוֹרֵשׁ מִמְּךָ כִּי אִם־עֲשׂוֹת מִשְׁפָּט וְאַהֲבַת חֶסֶד וְהַצְנֵעַ לֶכֶת עִם־אֱלֹקֶיךָ:

He has told you, O human, what is good,
And what the LORD requires of you.
And that is to do justice
And to love kindness,
And to walk modestly with your God. (Micah 6: 8)

I'd like to suggest that we can see a pattern here, starting with our relationship with God, moving towards our relationship with other people (which is founded in and shaped by our relationship with God), and then a movement back towards a focus on G again.

1. תָּמִים תִּהְיֶה עִם ה״ אֱלֹקיךָ:

You must be *tamim* with the LORD your God. (Dev. 18: 13)

What exactly does *tamim* mean? It's often translated as 'perfect' or 'complete'. The word appears in reference to calculating the date of Shavuot---we have to count seven *shabatot temimot*---i.e. whole, or complete weeks. Sacrifices too are often described as *tamim*---the animals must be whole, and not lack any limbs. But it need not mean 'perfect'. We also meet the word in connection with Noah, who is described as *tamim hayah bedorotav*---he was *tamim* in his generation. The midrash famously notes that he would not have been considered particularly virtuous in any other generation - but in his own context, he was indeed *tamim*. The New Jewish Publication Society translates the word as 'whole-hearted', and perhaps this gets to what is meant here: we are to be *complete* in our relationship with God. We may not be perfect, we may only be relatively good or virtuous, like Noah---but we have to develop a relationship with God that encompasses all of our being, the less ideal parts of us as well as those aspects that we feel proud of. We don't need to wait till we've got it all right---we just need to be wholly present, complete, *tamim*.

2. שִׁוִּיתִי ה״ לְנֶגְדִּי תָמִיד כִּי מִימִינִי בַּל־אֶמּוֹט;

I have placed the Lord always opposite me (Tehilim 16: 8)

Two words jump out at me here---*tamid*, 'always' and *lenegdi*---'opposite me', usually translated as 'before me'. 'Always' is a big ask---to be conscious of God all the time is something that is beyond us usually, but perhaps we can aspire to it for these

163

ten days---a sustained effort to live our lives in the presence of God. And not just 'in the presence' but 'opposite'---if we pick up on *lenegdi*, it implies that God is not just a passive presence, but is actively challenging us, to evaluate ourselves and our actions, to measure ourselves against God's moral system, not our own. Whether we relate to God as an unknowable cosmic presence or as the personal, emotional God of Tanakh, the moral demands that God makes are not always what we would choose, and not always convenient or comfortable.

The next verse takes us to a particularly difficult example, but one that has the potential to transform our lives.

3. ‏וְאָהַבְתָּ לְרֵעֲךָ כָּמוֹךָ אֲנִי ה'":‏

Love your fellow as yourself: I am the LORD. (Vayikra 19: 18)

From our relationship with God we move to our relationship with other humans, and are told to love them---again, not always something that is easy or comfortable. This is actually the second part of the verse: the first is '*Lo tikom velo titor et-benei amkha*'---You shall not take vengeance or bear a grudge against your people'. That most natural of responses---to remember our previous relationships and feelings about other people, based on their behaviour to us---is something that we have to move beyond, to a response of love. And the end of the verse tells us why: 'I am God'. Here too we are told to imitate God, as elsewhere we are told to 'be holy because I am holy'. And we are told that God's love does not depend on the virtues of those whom God loves---memorably, God tells us in Devarim (7: 7):

לֹא מֵרֻבְּכֶם מִכָּל־הָעַמִּים חָשַׁק ה״ בָּכֶם וַיִּבְחַר בָּכֶם כִּי־אַתֶּם הַמְעַט מִכָּל־הָעַמִּים:כִּי מֵאַהֲבַת ה״ אֶתְכֶם

'Not because you were more numerous than all the other peoples did God desire you and choose you, for you are the smallest of all the peoples, but because God loves you'.

Love does not always have to be for a reason, as we often find in our own experience. And apparently God wants us to extend that to other people.

Our next verse moves us back in the direction of God again.

4. : בְּכָל־דְּרָכֶיךָ דָעֵהוּ

In all your ways know Him (Mishlei 3: 6).

We are to try to know God in all our ways---those that involve interaction with other people, those where we are acting on our own---we need to work towards a consciousness of God, and an awareness of God's expectations of us. Again, a big ask, but something to keep as an aim towards which we are working. And that links to our last verse, which summarizes everything we have been thinking about so far:

5. הִגִּיד לְךָ אָדָם מַה־טּוֹב וּמָה־ה״ דּוֹרֵשׁ מִמְּךָ כִּי אִם־עֲשׂוֹת מִשְׁפָּט וְאַהֲבַת חֶסֶד וְהַצְנֵעַ לֶכֶת עִם־אֱלֹקֶיךָ:

He has told you, O human, what is good,
And what the LORD requires of you:
And that is to do justice
And to love goodness,
And to walk modestly with your God. (Micah 6: 8)

This is one of the classic expressions of the 'point of it all'---the aim of our Jewish lives. Interestingly it doesn't mention mitzvot, or the Temple and its sacrifices, or even Torah study, but focuses on the basic principles that God wants us to live by. God wants us to live with justice; with *hesed* (love or kindness), and to walk with God *hatsnea*---moderately, as well as we can, pushing ourselves to our own limits but not beyond them.

Together, we have a realistic and adaptable *teshuvah* programme here: to be wholly present, as much as we can be, in the presence of God; to try to base our relationships with other people on love that is as generous as that shown by God to us; to keep awareness of God's moral standards in all that we do, and to prize justice, *hesed*, and our continuing relationship with the divine, however we think of it. I wish us all much success in following this path.

Forgiving Others, Forgiving Ourselves

Rabbanit Sara Tillinger Wolkenfeld
Edited by Ronda Angel Arking

(previously published on Jofa.org)

Forgiveness is a complicated process. If you have ever been asked by another to forgive a serious offense, you will realize the enormity of what we are really asking from God. What does it mean to forgive? How do we envision this process of forgiveness, which we describe time and again during our prayer services on Yom Kippur?

Our liturgy alludes to the complexity of the forgiveness process. Perhaps the most familiar refrain of the High Holiday liturgy is the threefold request for absolution, found in the al het prayer. After cataloging and confessing all of our many transgressions, we beg our Creator:

> ועל כולם, אלוה סליחות- סלח לנו, מחל לנו, כפר לנו
> For all these, God of forgiveness — forgive us, pardon us, grant us atonement.

Each one of these three terms tells us something about the nature of the cycle of repentance and forgiveness. *Mehilah* is a technical, legal word, often used in the context of debts and loans. To be granted *mehilah* is to know that no debt is owed; no further consequences or punishment are forthcoming. Mehilah means that one may start over with a clean ledger.

Kapparah is most often translated as atonement, which implies something more sweeping

167

and restorative. To have successfully atoned is to have somehow made amends, or at least to have satisfied or appeased the offended party.

Selihah comes closest to the elusive quality of the English "forgiveness." It is the ultimate plea in a damaged relationship; *selihah* expresses the desire to repair what was harmed and be able to pick up where we left off, without the shadow of guilt or resentment.

Maimonides, in the second chapter of his Laws of Repentance, emphasizes that Yom Kippur atones only for sins between people and God.

אֵין הַתְּשׁוּבָה וְלֹא יוֹם הַכִּפּוּרִים מְכַפְּרִין אֶלָּא עַל עֲבֵרוֹת שֶׁבֵּין אָדָם לַמָּקוֹם כְּגוֹן מִי שֶׁאָכַל דָּבָר אָסוּר אוֹ בָּעַל בְּעִילָה אֲסוּרָה וְכַיּוֹצֵא בָּהֶן. אֲבָל עֲבֵרוֹת שֶׁבֵּין אָדָם לַחֲבֵרוֹ כְּגוֹן הַחוֹבֵל אֶת חֲבֵרוֹ אוֹ הַמְקַלֵּל חֲבֵרוֹ אוֹ גּוֹזְלוֹ וְכַיּוֹצֵא בָּהֶן אֵינוֹ נִמְחַל לוֹ לְעוֹלָם עַד שֶׁיִּתֵּן לַחֲבֵרוֹ מַה שֶּׁהוּא חַיָּב לוֹ וִירַצֵּהוּ. אַף עַל פִּי שֶׁהֶחֱזִיר לוֹ מָמוֹן שֶׁהוּא חַיָּב לוֹ צָרִיךְ לְרַצּוֹתוֹ וְלִשְׁאֹל מִמֶּנּוּ שֶׁיִּמְחַל לוֹ.

Repentance and the Day of Atonement atone only for sins between humans and God...but sins between people, such as one who injures another, or curses another, or robs him, and similar sins — these can never be completely absolved until one returns to one's friend what one owes, and appeases that person. Even if one returns all the money that is owed, one must still satisfy the other person and ask for pardon, even if one harmed another only through words, one must still appease that person and continue to contact that person until one is forgiven (Maimonides, Mishneh Torah, Laws of Repentance 2:9).

Even as we pour our hearts out to God and turn toward God's mercy, *Haza"l* impress upon us the need to keep our eyes and ears open for those around us who may be seeking our forgiveness.

We must apologize to those whom we have hurt or offended, and we must be ready to respond to those who have hurt us when they seek our pardon. The process Maimonides describes is as deep and complex between people as it is between people and God. We must first ensure *mehilah* by paying our debts and making any necessary reparations.

If the sin was a verbal jibe or emotional injury, we must somehow make amends and appease the person — that is, engage in *kapparah* — so that the offended party will be willing to wipe the slate clean. The intended result is that the other person will grant forgiveness; that differences will be overcome and rifts mended. Maimonides in the *Mishneh Torah* (Laws of Repentance 2:10) then adds:

אָסוּר לָאָדָם לִהְיוֹת אַכְזָרִי וְלֹא יִתְפַּיֵּס אֶלָּא יְהֵא נוֹחַ לִרְצוֹת וְקָשֶׁה לִכְעֹס וּבְשָׁעָה שֶׁמְּבַקֵּשׁ מִמֶּנּוּ הַחוֹטֵא לִמְחֹל מוֹחֵל בְּלֵב שָׁלֵם וּבְנֶפֶשׁ חֲפֵצָה.

It is forbidden for a person to be cruel, and not to be appeased. Rather, one should be easily satisfied, and difficult to anger.

When someone requests pardon, one should do so with a whole heart and a willing soul. Every individual is a link in the communal chain of atonement; you are required to ask forgiveness, and you are also required to forgive. When a person approaches another with sincere apology and remorse, it is cruel to withhold the pardon that we all seek at this time of year.

Rav Soloveitchik, as quoted in the book On Repentance, engages the difficulty of the process of repentance and forgiveness through a discussion of a famous Talmudic text. The Talmud in Yoma 86b suggests that through complete repentance, sins may be turned into merits. But how is such a thing possible? In Pinchas H. Peli's book *On Repentance: The Thought and Oral Discourses of Rabbi Joseph Dov Soloveitchik* (page 254), he writes that Rav Soloveitchik explains that when the process of repentance happens through love, the sin is integrated into the person one has become:

> Sin is not to be forgotten, blotted out, or cast into the depths of the sea. On the contrary, sin has to be remembered. It is the memory of sin that releases the power within the inner depths of the soul of the penitent to do greater things than ever before.

I believe this same idea may be applied to forgiveness on an interpersonal level. In most cases, Rabbi Soloveitchik argued, there is no possibility of forgetting what has come before — nor would we want to excise whole portions of ourselves and our experiences. "Forgive and forget" is not a Jewish idea, nor is it generally a realistic expectation. Traumas are not easily forgotten, and memory is often essential to a mature friendship. Remembering can lead to resentment, pain, and distance — o rit can deepen a relationship. The Talmud is not teaching us that our sins are really "for the best," but rather, that the process of sinning and repenting has propelled us forward on the road of life. Our experiences have given us a new perspective, and we are ready to move on with life. Forgiveness is an essential process in all relationships. Not only does one not forget — on the contrary, it is important to remember, and memories give life and relationships depth and texture.

There is an additional aspect to this practice of supplication and atonement: the process of forgiving ourselves. How do I know that God has forgiven me? We can never know for certain, but after weeks of prayerful apology, we hope to have achieved a closeness to God that cultivates within us a certain religious confidence. We can never know for certain the effects of our prayers, but we need that religious confidence in order to see ourselves advancing on the path toward spiritual perfection. To make this year better, more fruitful and more elevated, than last year, we need to let go — not of the memories, nor even of the residue of the pain of last year — but of resentment, of anxiety, of "debts." We need to resolve to change, to do something different when faced with the same situation. Only then can we stand in the presence of true *selihah*, of forgiveness.

May we merit complete *selihah*, *mehilah*, and *kapparah*, from God, from each other, and from ourselves.

Hannah's Prayer:
A Rosh Hashana D'var Torah

Sandra E. Rapoport

Words are our tools. We are, after all, known as the People of the Book; Moses sums up a lifetime of serving God and leading Israel in the Book of Devarim, meaning "the book of words." Yet, years earlier, at the Burning Bush, when Moses had tried to convince God that he was not fit to be God's representative to Pharaoh, Moses had cried, *"Lo ish devarim anochi."* "I am *not* a man of words. Choose someone more eloquent than I." As if to say, verbal skill is a prime qualifier for a hero or a leader.

And of course, the Ten Commandments, the most important outline of laws-to-live-by in the history of mankind, [Exod. 20:2-17] are known in the Bible as *Aseret HaDibrot*, the ten utterances, or spoken words.

So we would be forgiven if we forgot, momentarily, that even silent unspoken prayer — delivered directly to God —is revered in Judaism. So much so, that it is at the center of our Rosh Hashana and High Holiday worship.

Think of the *Amidah*, the eighteen-prayer centerpiece of not only our High Holiday prayers, but of the daily prayers, too. The lengthy *Amidah* prayer—a prayer that uses the rabbis' timeless poetic words—is recited in a whisper, processed, as it is, individually, in each of our minds and hearts, intentionally directed into God's ears. With the utmost respect and affection for Rabbi Shlomo Carlebach, who sang his prayers, it is the *Amidah's* whispered, personal prayer that endures as the Jewish prototype.

Jewish prayer in general, and particularly on the High Holidays, is modeled on the anguished, respectful and partially *unvoiced* prayer of one Biblical woman: Hannah, barren and righteous wife of Elkanah, an Israelite living at the time of the Temple in Shiloh, in the years before Israel had a king.

The Haftarah reading for the first day of Rosh Hashana [1 Sam. 1-2] tells Hannah's story. This is fitting, because Rosh Hashana is the Jewish Day of Remembrance, [TB Rosh Hashana 11a] and Hannah's story tells of God "remembering" an infertile woman, ending her barrenness. We consider this single act of divine memory to be a microcosm of God remembering all of humanity.

The book of Samuel chronologically follows the book of Shoftim, the book of Judges, which chronicles a violent, and mostly non-God-fearing, century-and-a-half of Israelite history.

Samuel opens with the detailed description of the dishonest and immoral behavior of two Israelite priests, sons of the saintly Eli, the elderly priest at the Temple in Shiloh. It is into this fraught situation — where everyone, even priests, act the way they wish, and the words of God are ignored — that Hannah is introduced.

As was the case with the matriarch Sarah in Genesis 11:30, one of the first facts we are told about Hannah is that she is barren. Also, though Hannah is Elkanah's first (and favored) wife, it is Elkanah's second wife who is the fertile one, bearing Elkanah children, and tormenting Hannah.

The haftarah is quietly thrilling. We recognize the narrative trope; we have seen it before, with Sarah and Rachel: the

173

beloved barren wife, the fertile rival wife, and the existential agony of infertility shading the barren wife's every living moment. But this time we anticipate that the Tanakh will perhaps add something important to the familiar story. So we read on.

The drama is intense. We read that time sits heavily on Hannah's shoulders. Year after year Elkanah brings his entire family to Shiloh to offer ritual sacrifices, and though Hannah surely has prayed to God to open her womb, she remains childless, in the face of her rival wife's fecundity. We can literally feel Hannah's deep despair, along with the excruciatingly slow passing of infertile time.

> This time, though, Hannah takes the initiative, and makes a vow to God: "O Lord of Hosts, if You remember me and do not forget your maidservant, but (instead) give me a male child, I will in turn give him to the Lord all the days of his life, nor will a razor come upon his head." [1 Sam. 1:11]

This is extraordinary. Hannah is unique in the Tanakh; she initiates prayer and prays to God. "Unlike the matriarchs, Hannah has to take matters into her own hands and approach God personally." [Rabbi David Silber, *Tanach Companion, The Book of Samuel*, "The Birth of Samuel and the Birth of Kingship," p.15]

Further, in the Bible, a sincere vow to God is a powerful thing. It is a holy obligation between God and the one making the vow, and it is binding. Hannah has silently vowed that any future son would be marked as a *Nazir*, his hair unshorn, and his life one of service to God. It is this sincere vow, uttered *silently* from the depth of Hannah's soul, that God hears, but that Eli, the old priest of Shiloh, misconstrues.

The Tanakh tells us the story of Hannah's silent prayer/vow to God, painting a vivid picture of her agony. Hannah has prostrated herself in the Temple. Silent tears drip from her chin. Her eyes are closed tight, and her mouth moves in silent entreaty.

> "And Hannah spoke in her heart; only her lips moved, but her voice was not heard." [1 Sam. 1:13, Underlined emphasis is added.]

To the priest's eyes, Hannah appears to be drunk. So Eli approaches Hannah, and excoriates her.

> "How long will you be a drunkard? Put away your wine, and leave these holy precincts!" [1 Sam. 1:14]

We hear Hannah's voice for the first time now, as she responds to Eli. We think, is it audacious for Hannah to speak thus to the priest of Shiloh? Or is she justified, heroic and desperate to speak up?

Perhaps God is listening.

> "No, my lord," says Hannah, "I am not a drunkard. I have drunk no wine or other strong drink. I am a woman of sorrowful spirit. I have poured out my soul before the Lord. Take not your maidservant to be a worthless woman, for it is out of my great complaint and grief that I have been speaking." [1 Sam. 1:15-16]

We note that Hannah has not revealed to the old priest what she is beseeching of God. After Hannah's response, Eli is chastened. In his defense, Eli has never before come upon a truly devout Israelite at prayer in the Temple at Shiloh; certainly never a woman! [D. Silber, *loc. cit.*, p.13] So it is Eli who blinks. He recognizes in Hannah's demeanor and eloquence a genuine righteousness, perhaps a spark of greatness. Instead of the rebuke he had begun to utter, he sends Hannah off with an implicit apology, [TB Berakhot31b] a strong blessing, and a prophecy ringing in her ears.

> "*Lechi l'shalom!* Go in peace. The God of Israel will grant you the petition you have asked of Him." [1 Sam. 1:17]

Hannah's heart lightens, so strong is her belief in the old priest's words. And, in fact, we are told that God remembers Hannah, and she becomes pregnant, and delivers a boy child. [1 Sam. 1:19-20]

When the boy is two years old [Rashi] and is weaned, Hannah fulfills her vow and brings her son to Eli at the Temple, reminding Eli that she is the woman he mistook for a drunkard three years before, and that this was the son for whom she had prayed silently to God that day. At his birth, Hannah had named the boy *Shmuel*, "because I have asked God for him." [1 Sam. 21] *Shmu-El* in Hebrew can also mean "God has heard" — and answered — my prayers.

Hannah explains to Eli that she is keeping her part of the vow, and is hereby presenting her son to Eli to raise in service to God. Rashi [1 Sam. 1:26] adds that Hannah not only was giving her son to Eli to be his lifelong pupil; she also was charging Eli to keep the boy safe from all harm.

As chapter 1 closes, Hannah, her husband Elkanah, and the boy Samuel prostrate themselves before God.

Chapter 2 opens with the words "*Vatitpalel Chanah, vatomer.*" "And Hannah prayed, and she said..." And for ten full verses [1 Sam. 2:1-10] we read Hannah's second prayer to God.

176

It is not clear whether this prayer is also silent, as was the one in chapter 1. But regardless, it is poetic, powerful and prophetic, reminding the reader of Deborah's *shirah*, her song of thanksgiving, in chapter 5 of the preceding book of Judges. The Tanakh is implicitly raising Hannah to the level of Deborah and Miriam, her eloquent biblical forebears.

Listen to her words:

> "My heart rejoices in the Lord!
> …There is none as holy as the Lord;
> There is no rock like our God…
> Let not arrogance come out of your mouth…
> Bows of the mighty men are broken;
> Those who stumbled are girded with strength.
> …Those who were hungry ceased to hunger;
> <u>the barren woman has borne seven</u>…"
> [Underlined emphasis is added.]

We parse Hannah's prayer. First, she eloquently acknowledges God's sovereignty. This is fitting to read on Rosh Hashana, when the major theme of the day is *Malchiyot*, God's kingship. Only when Hannah is at the halfway mark does she make her personal point. She attests, in effect, that "Nothing is beyond Your ability, O Lord! Only You can reverse Nature! Only You could open a barren woman's womb."

Hannah juxtaposes herself to the hungry man whom God has fed. Her meaning is clear. "Fulfilling my hunger for a child is as poignant and life-affirming as Your giving food to a starving man." Giving me a son has kept me alive and has assured my immortality.

Nothing is impossible for the Lord, Hannah is saying.

And we recognize our modern-day prayers (notably our Hallel prayer) in Hannah's classic poetic duality:

> "The Lord kills, and returns to life...
> The Lord makes poor and makes rich;
> He brings low and He lifts up.
> He raises up the poor from the dust,
> and lifts up the beggar from the dunghill,
> To set them among princes,
> and to make them inherit the throne of glory...
> He will keep the feet of His pious ones...
> The adversaries of the Lord shall be broken to pieces...
> The Lord shall judge the ends of the earth, and
> <u>He shall give strength to His king,</u>
> <u>and exalt the horn of His anointed.</u>"
> [Underlined emphasis is added.]

Hannah's words go further than just an eloquent prayer of praise and thanksgiving. In fact, her final couplet is perhaps the primary reason the rabbis of the Talmud name Hannah as one of the Bible's seven prophetesses. [TB Meg.14a]

This is because in the very last phrases of her prayer Hannah does the unprecedented. <u>She predicts an Israelite monarchy.</u> God will anoint a king over Israel, she says.

This is momentous. It is Hannah, then, this erstwhile barren, distraught woman who against all reason retained her faith in a God who listens, who now predicts a sovereign Israel under God. She even envisions the horn of holy oil anointing God's chosen king.

These ten verses are a tour-de-force poem praising God's power. Hannah here has issued a personal and a communal blessing of praise and thanksgiving, as well as a prophecy of a future Israelite monarchy. Hannah's strong words ring true because she is certain they will be fulfilled. She is a living witness. After all, God has heard *her* prayers.

And we recognize the sweet, dramatic irony of her words of prophecy. It will, in fact, be her son Samuel who, years into the future, will anoint both the first and second kings chosen by God to lead Israel.

Hannah is the undisputed heroine of chapters 1 and 2 of Samuel. Her words of prayer—words of desperation, vow, and ultimately praise and prophecy—illuminate the way for all Israel to pray to God three millennia later.

So we remember Hannah, and God's fulfillment of her prayers, as we open our hearts in prayer this Rosh Hashana.

Sandra E. Rapoport is an attorney, a Bible teacher, and the award-winning author of four books on Torah and Midrash.

Transitions: Holding Grief and Joy Together

Dahlia Topolsky, PsyD

This summer, and especially as we start the academic year, I have been thinking about transitions. Three out of four of our children are going through major milestones this year. Our eldest son, who just returned from his gap year in Israel, just started college. Our 17-year-old son is now a senior, applying to college and gap year programs, and will be graduating in February. As part of his school's program, he will then be heading to Israel for three months. Our 14-year-old daughter just started high school. And while our youngest daughter (age 12) isn't going through any major transition, she just started 7th grade and has most definitely been feeling the changes happening around her, as our family continues to adapt to these very natural next stages.

As a psychologist, I am constantly working with clients going through key life changes, both joyous ones and painful ones. I am giving support, offering tools, and helping many processes and navigate whatever transitions they may face such as starting college, graduating, finding a job, moving, getting married, ending a relationship, mourning the loss of a loved one, becoming a parent, etc. I share with my clients that even the most joyous stages of life are often accompanied by both grief and celebration. When one gets married, they are filled with so much happiness and excitement, yet simultaneously there may be sadness and a grieving of the childhood they are leaving behind, a lost sense of individuality, and/or a shift of identity as they now enter the shared space of marriage. While it's sometimes easier to put things into black and white categories, the reality is that even positive change comes along with a complexity of emotions that are very real and important to feel and acknowledge.

Similarly, as we experience the Jewish months of Elul and Tishrei, the opportunity for teshuva (repentance), serves as a transition to the Jewish New Year. For many, there is joy in second chances and hopes for self-growth, to aspire to be your true self; there is great excitement as you anticipate the potential of what the new year may bring. But it's also true that taking the time for self-reflection can invoke deep feelings of sadness for what has been lost and missed.

Understanding the meaning of the sounds of the shofar that we blow during these months reflects the emotional experience that we often feel during life transitions. There are three different types of noises that are sounded when we blow the shofar: The "tekiah," a long continuous blast, "shevarim," three short blasts, and the "teruah," a set of nine short blasts. The Gemara in Rosh Hashana (33b) explains that the shevarim and teruah sounds are meant to sound like crying: ". . . drawing a long sigh. . . uttering short piercing cries." I recently read an explanation by the Ben Ish Chai that these crying sounds are deliberately meant to contrast with the tekiah. The tekiah, the long blast, is a sound of triumph and joy, reminiscent in the torah of the coronation of the King. Every year, during Rosh Hashana, we celebrate as Hashem is crowned King of the universe and we acknowledge that the mitzvot are for the good of humankind. In contrast, according to the gemara, the sounds of the shevarim, which translates as fractured/broken, and the teruah, as explained by the Targum as a "yevavah," a broken, crying sound, are both sounds of pain.

Thus when we hear the shofar, we are meant to be simultaneously holding joy and pain together as we go into the new year. Rather than view this as negative, the sounds of the shofar acknowledge and reflect the complexity of emotions that we feel as human beings as we go through transitions. The shofar gives us permission to grieve, while at the same time, reminds us that we have hope and much to celebrate. It teaches us that we have the ability to anticipate the newness while also recognizing and honoring what has transpired.

As we end the shofar blasts with one long tekiah gedola, may we be reminded that we are whole beings that experience the complexity of human emotion, the loss and the incredible gains at each stage of life.

Yom Kippur

A New Guide to Viduy (Yom Kippur)

Rachel Anisfeld

(originally published at https://rachelanisfeld.com/2021/09/14/commentary-a-new-guide-to-viduy-yom-kippur/)

Teshuva, repentance, has three interfaces — God, other and self. We tend to emphasize the first two and think little of the third. Yet the three are inextricably linked; we will make only incomplete progress in the other two arenas if we don't invest in our relationship to ourselves.

I want to look at the sins enumerated in the *viduy*, the repeated confession of Yom Kippur, and read them in relation to the self. Note that most of the sins described, with only a few exceptions, do not name an object, but are generalized attitudes that can be applied to any object, including oneself.

Below I proceed alphabetically, picking out some representatives from the list of *al het*'s as examples of how this type of interpretation might work:

עַל חֵטְא שֶׁחָטָאנוּ לְפָנֶיךָ . . .

For the sins we have sinned before You . . .

בבלי דעת

"Unwittingly" — *Our sins against ourselves are often unconscious, born of long ingrained habits of self-reproach and aggression. How can we begin to notice the patterns, to pause at that triggering moment when we begin to turn on ourselves and to make a different choice?*

185

בדבור פה

"Through the words of our mouth" (one of many related to speech) — *How have we sinned against ourselves in the way that we speak to ourselves? What insults and meanness have we hurled inside that we would never think to say to someone else?*

בחזק יד

"Through force" — *How have we used force inside in a harsh, uncompassionate way — notice all the "should"s in your system — demanding that we measure up to self-imposed standards, forcing change and productivity in a cold no-nonsense way? See how much suffering force causes inside — exhaustion and restlessness and a sense of inadequacy — and how it tramples on joy and the natural unfolding of the self. What are some ways we might motivate and move forward without the harshness and pressure of constant force?*

בחלול השם

"Through the desecration of Your name" — *How have we failed to honor the divine aspect of ourselves and thereby desecrated God's name as well as our own?*

בכחש ובכזב

"Through deceit and lies" — *What are some of the false beliefs about ourselves that lie hidden inside, subtly undergirding our daily motivations and actions — such as the belief in our unworthiness or inadequacy or not mattering, the belief in our need to earn love and our very existence, the belief in our capacity to control everything, and the belief in our essential aloneness and separateness? How can we come to see that these are untrue, that, in their falseness, they, too, are a kind of sin, causing suffering and harm inside as well as outside of us?*

בכפת שחד

"Through bribery" — *What inner bribes have we agreed to take in order not to see truth or feel pain? What comfort or addiction have we used to cover over something we don't want to feel?*

בלצון

"Through scorn" — *Which parts of ourselves do we scorn and mock and treat disparagingly?*

במאכל ובמשתה

"Through food and drink" — *How have we sinned against ourselves through eating and drinking? How have we harmed our divinely created bodies? How have we caused ourselves to suffer through too much control and judgment around food, or used food or drink as a way not to feel what needs to be felt?*

בעיניים רמות

"Through haughty eyes" — *Sometimes we sin against ourselves through pride, by thinking that we need praise in order to matter, by pursuing ambition in order to protect the parts of us that don't feel worthy — thereby only perpetuating the cycle, temporarily filling the hole, but further strengthening the notion that we need such praise in order to matter in the world. How can we hold our sense of center steadily, with equanimity, through both praise and blame, pride and shame?*

בפריקת עול

"By casting off the yoke" — *We regularly cast off the yoke of our commitment to ourselves, our commitment to taking care of our needy parts, our responsibility to listen and attend and be true to ourselves. How many times have we abandoned ourselves in our neediest moments, rejecting instead of nurturing at the very moments when we needed the nurturing most? When we throw off the yoke of caring for ourselves, we also throw off the yoke of the God who gave us this one precious life to live and enjoy and be true,*

בפלילות
"Through judgment" — *See how we judge ourselves so harshly, how the inner critic finds constant fault, not favor, with what we do, who we are, what we say. Surely this harshness is a sin against ourselves and the many suffering parts of us that need not judgment, but love. We ask for forgiveness for this inner critic, so that even this tendency to judge ourselves may be wrapped in a blanket of divine compassion on this day.*

בריצת רגליים להרע
"Through running to evil" — *We run away from what we are feeling; we don't stay and tend and allow and feel. And this running away — towards something we think will save us but never does, or if it does, does so only temporarily — this running away hurts us, makes our neediness feel abandoned; adds another layer to our suffering, an aloneness. How have we sinned against ourselves by running and not staying, and how can we learn to stay, to stay with what is, to stay with what aches, not to fix and heal — another kind of running — but just to stay.*

בשנאת חנם
"Through baseless hatred" — *How often have we sinned against ourselves through hatred — falling into the trance of self-aversion or self-loathing, seeing ourselves through an ugly prism that distorts and misshapes until we are so sick of ourselves we sometimes wish we could disappear? Notice the hatred turned inward, how heavy*

188

and baseless and debilitating. We ask for forgiveness for this sin because it, too, no, it, especially, is a sin before the God who made us as we are.

בתמהון לבב

"Through confusion of the heart" — *Confusion often comes to obfuscate the way to an open heart, in order to protect us from fully feeling whatever pain has arrived. It is a running away, another form of self-abandonment. We hold it, too, in compassion, but ask for forgiveness for the additional suffering it causes, for its role in blocking the way to clarity and truth and an alive heart.*

For all of these, O Lord of Forgiveness, we ask for forgiveness. We ask You to hold all these harmful tendencies in Your abundant loving kindness, and to help us, too, learn to hold them — and all of humanity — in that larger space of love, the river of forgiveness that wants to wash over us all on this day.

Dunk Your Shame in Hope
(Yom Kippur)
Rachel Anisfeld

(originally published on https://rachelanisfeld.com/2022/10/03/short-essay-dunk-your-shame-in-hope-yom-kippur/)

אָמַר רַבִּי עֲקִיבָא, אַשְׁרֵיכֶם יִשְׂרָאֵל, לִפְנֵי מִי אַתֶּם מִטַּהֲרִין, וּמִי מְטַהֵר
אֶתְכֶם, אֲבִיכֶם שֶׁבַּשָּׁמַיִם, שֶׁנֶּאֱמַר (יחזקאל לו), וְזָרַקְתִּי עֲלֵיכֶם מַיִם
טְהוֹרִים וּטְהַרְתֶּם. וְאוֹמֵר (ירמיה יז), מִקְוֵה יִשְׂרָאֵל ה', מַה מִּקְוֶה מְטַהֵר
אֶת הַטְּמֵאִים, אַף הַקָּדוֹשׁ בָּרוּךְ הוּא מְטַהֵר אֶת יִשְׂרָאֵל

God is our mikvah, says Rabbi Akiva in this last mishnah of tractate Yoma (8:9). God is our cleansing agent, our healing agent. On Yom Kippur we look at ourselves in all our messiness, and we place ourselves, naked and vulnerable and full of shame, into the healing waters of God, the only container that can truly hold us as we are, and we somehow emerge – as from a mikvah – purified and whole and renewed for the year ahead.

Rabbi Akiva bases his mikvah analogy on a phrase in Jeremiah – מִקְוֵה יִשְׂרָאֵל ה, *mikveh Yisrael Hashem*, which literally means "The Lord is the Hope of Israel (Jeremiah 17:13)," but which Rabbi Akiva reads as: "The Lord is the mikvah – the ritual bath – of Israel," based on the double meaning of the biblical word *mikveh*, which can either denote "hope" or "collected body of water."

This is not as radical an interpretation of the phrase as it would seem at first glance, as the end of the verse speaks of God as *mekor mayim hayim,* "the Fount of living waters" so that an association between water and God is already very much a part of the verse.

There is more. The second phrase of this same verse is *kol ozvekha yevoshu*, which literally means "all who forsake You shall be put to shame," and the word for shame, *yevoshu*, is similar to another word related to water (or lack thereof), *yavesh*, "dry." In other words, those who forsake the Fount of Living Waters become shamed, by which we mean "dried out" in some way, because of their loss of connection to these nourishing waters.

Putting this all together and keeping both meanings of *mikveh* and *yevoshu* alive at once, we might say that the verse, according to Rabbi Akiva, has the following message: Dunk your Shame in divine Hope, so that your dried out-ness, your deadness, will be re-invigorated by the waters of the living God.

Dunk your Shame in divine Hope. Shame can lead to despair. It can indeed be a path of dryness, of lifelessness; it can be so debilitating that it robs a person of any possibility of change or movement or healing or transformation. Shame eats at who we are, tells us not just that we have done stupid or terrible things, but also that we *are* stupid and terrible, that we are worthless, that we amount to nothing and are nothing. We can get lost and stuck in this place, overcome by hopelessness, collapsed in on ourselves by the weight of the shame we carry.

But what happens if we dunk our shame in divine hope, if we take the feeling of worthlessness that is sometimes at our core, that dries us up and shrivels us and robs us of a will to live and thrive, what happens if we dunk that feeling into a ritual bath that is full of the divine waters of hope, the hope that God is still with us, that we actually can change, that we are in fact created in God's image and essentially good at our very core and that it is therefore always possible to uncover and return to that goodness, to that essential value, the hope that we are

191

never a lost cause, never too damaged for repair, the hope that God still loves us and cares about us and will help us evolve and manifest, will hold us and support us in the gentle waters of divine kindness like a baby in its mother's womb, swaddled and held until we are ready to emerge again, renewed by our contact with the eternal Fount of living waters?

Mikveh, Hope, is a powerful healing agent, if – like an impure person in the mikvah waters – we fully immerse ourselves in it, we let ourselves be surrounded by its strength and confidence and faith in our capacity for wholeness. Shame is the sureness that we are essentially worthless, a turning away from ourselves and the possibility of something more. Hope is the knowledge of what we could be and the energy and vision to move in that direction. Hope fuels change and healing. When we fully submerge in these waters of possibility, feeling the support of a loving eternal God who believes in us, then we come more fully to believe in ourselves; the waters cleanse our view of ourselves so that we emerge not just more whole, but also *seeing ourselves* as more whole, cleansed of the shame that drags us into the downward spiral of despair. Hope purifies us by allowing us to see who we are and who we could become.

This Yom Kippur, dunk your Shame in the mikvah of divine Hope.

Yonah's Growing Pains
Ilana Gimpelevich, Richmond, VA

Summer has been good to my garden, showering my family with bountiful produce. My personal favorite vegetables are the tomatoes that sprouted from last year's crop. In gardening circles these plants are referred to as volunteers: the seeds scattered by the squirrels and the birds last fall that laid dormant and grew on their own. The red skin of the cherry tomatoes glistens in the sun. All I have to do is enter the garden, pick the fruit, and rejoice that I did not plant it, or tend it, but here it is, ready for my enjoyment.

As a gardener, there is some perverse satisfaction in reaping the rewards of a plant that one did not have to care for. My delight parallels that of Yonah over the mysterious plant, the kikayon (gourd or squash) that grew practically overnight.

וַיְמַן יְהֹוָה־אֱלֹהִים קִיקָיוֹן וַיַּעַל מֵעַל לְיוֹנָה לִהְיוֹת צֵל עַל־רֹאשׁוֹ לְהַצִּיל לוֹ מֵרָעָתוֹ וַיִּשְׂמַח יוֹנָה עַל־הַקִּיקָיוֹן שִׂמְחָה גְדוֹלָה:

(6) Hashem, God, appointed a kikayon and it rose up above Yonah to be a shade upon his head, to save him from his evil. And Yonah was very glad about the kikayon.
(Yonah 4:6)

On the macro level, the story of Yonah and the kikayon is a snapshot in Yonah's drama involving the sinful city of Ninveh. G-d commands him to prophesy to the city a warning that it is about to be destroyed for its evil deeds. Yonah acts erratically: first by fleeing from his mission and from the potential to save human life, then, after a stint in the belly of the fish, by fulfilling his mission. The city of Ninveh carries out the repentance by fasting and donning sackcloth and ashes on all the inhabitants, including the cattle. Hashem sees the actions of the city and forgives the city. The city is saved from רָעָה, evil (3:10).

The destruction of G-d's creations, even if they deserved it, is perceived as evil in G-d's eyes. The book of Yonah could have ended after the third chapter, with an example of a successful teshuva (repentance).

Yet there is a mysterious chapter four, the one containing the story of Yonah and the kikayon. Curiously, it starts out with Yonah feeling that it was evil of G-d not to destroy Ninveh. Yonah is questioning G-d's morality. He cannot comprehend the instruments of repentance and begs not to stay alive in the world that is not ruled by the strict attributes of justice. G-d's response is baffling:

(ד) וַיֹּאמֶר יְהֹוָה הַהֵיטֵב חָרָה לָךְ:

(Literally:) And Hashem said: is it better that you are angry? (Yonah 4:4)

Ibn Ezra and Targum Yonatan rely on the Aramaic reading of "tuva": Are you very angry?

Yonah does not respond but storms out of the city, and places himself to the east, as a spectator. One gets a sense that Yonah feels that he made a compelling argument for G-d to act strictly and mete out the punishment that the city deserved, whether it repented or not. Alternatively, Yonah, by being angry with G-d, is acting in a way that would draw Divine wrath upon him and away from the city. He is acting as a petulant child, pushing the boundary. Yonah had explicitly stated his death wish and his behavior is congruent with someone welcoming a suicide by G-d's anger.

At this very moment, a kikayon appears to diffuse the tension. Yonah, who is expecting imminent destruction either of himself, or of the city's inhabitants, is distracted by the sheer joy that a simple plant brings to his wait. The kikayon is there to לְהַצִּיל לוֹ מֵרָעָתוֹ, "save him from his evil" (4:6). Just as I was delighted in my volunteer tomatoes, so is Yonah smitten with the kikayon. While the text focuses on the physical comforts that the plant brings to the prophet, I am left to wonder whether Yonah also contemplated the sudden undeserved bounty that sprouted overnight. It does not fit into his rigid framework of reward and punishment. Strictly, Yonah does not deserve this plant, not after his behavior. Its appearance upends the rigidity of the rules of fairness, forcing Yonah to consider whether he himself would like to inhabit the world where one gets exactly what one deserves. He is forced to reconsider how this unbidden plant can show him a different path forward and save him from his rigid thoughts.

As the seasons go, the warm summer days will give way to the cooler breaths of the fall. The leaves will turn yellow and wither, and the summer bounty will diminish until one morning when there will not be a vegetable in sight. There is a season for all: a time to grow and a time to harvest, a time of bounty and a time of scarcity, as Kohelet declares (Chapter 3). Yet there is a nemesis that destroys the vines overnight, before their time: the vine borer. All of a sudden, one awakes to droopy leaves and a dying plant, with a telltale pile of sawdust on the vine. There are preventative treatments, but once the borer has taken hold, the best remedy is to pull the dying vine out, and not to plant squash in the same spot the following year.

I am left to wonder whether Yonah's "worm", תּוֹלַעַת, was such a vine borer, killing the shady vine overnight (4:7). The kikayon elevates Yonah's spirits to such an extent that he is unable to process its sudden loss. He is even more despondent over the loss of the plant that he was over the potential loss of human life. Ironically, it is Yonah who echoes G-d's previous words in his response:

וַיֹּאמֶר הֵיטֵב חָרָה־לִי עַד־מָוֶת

"And he said: I am very angry, to the point of death", or, "It is better for me to be this angry". (Yonah 4:9)

G-d's response in the final two pesukim is illuminating. He reminds Yonah that the prophet had no stake in the sudden blossoming of the kikayon: he did not plant it, tend to it, worry about it, pin any hopes and dreams to it. Yet, he is as aggrieved over its demise as a farmer who invested a lot of time and effort in the crop. Yonah is a stand-in for Hashem, who is the One aggrieved both by the death of the kikayon and by the potential death of the thousands of the inhabitants of Ninveh. In this sublime lesson, Hashem also lets it slip that Yonah is as much part of the Divine plan as the kikayon and the populous city. Yonah's constant belief that he can invite death upon himself with his erratic behavior and disobedience flies in the face of Hashem's appreciation that everything, even a petulant prophet, is deserving of mercy, compassion, dialogue, and a pathway of teshuva.

As for me, I will return to savoring the sudden bounty of cherry tomatoes and try not to mourn too hard on that morning when they inevitably will be gone.

What Does Queen Esther Have to Do with the High Holidays?

Sharona Halickman

In each of the High Holiday prayer services, we recite the word "u'vchen", "and so…" Avudraham points out that the word "u'vchen" was also used by Queen Esther as she prepared to go to go before King Achashverosh in Megillat Ester, 4:15-16: Then Esther said to reply to Mordechai: "Go assemble all the Jews that are to be found in Shushan, and fast for me; do not eat or drink for three days, night or day: And I, with my maids will fast also, and so (u'vchen) I will go to the king, though it is against the law: and if I perish, I perish."

As we stand before God, the Supreme king of kings, we begin with the same word that Esther uttered before standing before the human king, Achashverosh.

The Siddur, Magid Tzedek explains that if Esther who had fasted for three days in penitence and prayer in preparation for her appearance before the king was still terribly frightened, then we too should remember the sacrifices that Esther made and tremble in awe in the presence of God.

Rabbi Abraham Besdin adapted Rabbi Joseph B. Soloveitchik's teachings in the book Reflections of the Rav. In the section called "The Dual Character of Purim", the Rav teaches that "Purim is also a day of introspection and prayerful meditation. The Megillah is both a Book of Distress and Petition.

The narrative relates two stories of a people in a terrifying predicament and also their great exhilaration at their sudden deliverance."

The Rav goes on to say that Taanit Esther which is commemorated the day before Purim through fasting, Slichot and the recitation of the Avinu Malkeinu prayer sets the mood of solemn penitence. It reflects the fear of the Jews on the 13th of Adar as they fought their enemies. Purim day celebrates the victory and the sudden miraculous salvation of the Jewish people.

The Rav concludes: "Perhaps the feature common to both Purim and Yom Kippur is that aspect of Purim which is a call for Divine compassion and intercession, a mood of petition arising from great distress."

Let us hope and pray that just as God answered the prayers of the Jewish people in the days of Ester, so too will He listen to our Yom Kippur prayers and seal us in the Book of Life.

Then Shall Your Light Shine in the Darkness

Daphne Lazar Price
Edited by Ronda Arking

(previously published on Jofa.org)

Jewish life is replete with halakhic obligations and rituals that serve both the individual and the community and are conducted both in private and in public. How do these two realms relate to one another? Being a part of a community is an important value, as is recognizing and finding ways to support the marginalized among us. This is evident from the *birkhot haShahar*, the morning blessings, when we express gratitude for God's benevolence in helping the blind to see, enabling the feeble to walk, providing clothing for the poor, and freeing those in captivity.

Throughout our calendar year, there are moments when we step out of the mundane and into more holy and heady days. In preparation for the *Yamim Nora'im*, the High Holidays, at the start of the month of Elul, it is customary to blow the shofar at the end of Shaharit, the morning services, sounding out the tekiah, shevarim, teruah, and tekiah/teruah gedolah calls. The cry of the shofar is jarring, haunting. The prophet Amos asks, "Can a shofar be blown in the city and the people not tremble?"

The *Aseret Yemei Teshuva* mark the Ten Days of Repentance that start with Rosh Hashana and culminate with Yom Kippur, when we shift our focus toward self-awareness asking for and offering forgiveness to one another in an effort to achieve true repentance. It is traditional to increase Torah learning and to mindfully modify our behaviors as a nod toward the gravity of Yom Kippur.

The liturgy and practices on Yom Kippur are intended to intensify our own personal connection to the day. In contrast to a typical day, Shabbat, or Yom Tov, we refrain from eating and drinking, wearing leather shoes, bathing, applying lotions, and having marital relations. The prayer services are filled with references to worship at the *mishkan* (sanctuary), and several times throughout the day we stand, heads bowed, reciting the al het ("for our sins") prayers of atonement as we beat on our hearts. It is a serious day; a constant reminder that our individual fates are inscribed on Rosh Hashana, and then sealed on Yom Kippur. We have no choice but to be introspective.

On Yom Kippur morning, our Torah reading focuses exclusively on ritual behavior specifically, the prescribed worship on Yom Kippur in the *mishkan* (Leviticus 16:134). Traditionally, the haftarah readings are thematically related to the Torah reading; but the Yom Kippur haftarah, surprisingly, seems to contradict the Torah reading almost entirely pronouncing ritual to be meaningless in the eyes of God. These passages serve as a reminder almost a rebuke not to separate ritual practice from realities dictated by social and moral considerations. The haftarah reminds us of the human condition:

הֵן לְרִיב וּמַצָּה֙ תָּצ֔וּמוּ וּלְהַכּ֖וֹת בְּאֶגְרֹ֣ף רֶ֑שַׁע לֹא־תָצ֣וּמוּ כַיּ֔וֹם לְהַשְׁמִ֥יעַ בַּמָּר֖וֹם קוֹלְכֶֽם׃

Because you fast in strife and contention, And you strike with a wicked fist! Your fasting today is not suchAs to make your voice heard on high.

הֲכָזֶ֗ה יִֽהְיֶה֙ צ֣וֹם אֶבְחָרֵ֔הוּ י֛וֹם עַנּ֥וֹת אָדָ֖ם נַפְשׁ֑וֹ הֲלָכֹ֨ף כְּאַגְמֹ֤ן רֹאשׁוֹ֙ וְשַׂ֤ק וָאֵ֙פֶר֙ יַצִּ֔יעַ הֲלָזֶ֙ה֙ תִּקְרָא־צ֔וֹם וְי֥וֹם רָצ֖וֹן לַיהֹוָֽה׃

Is such the fast I desire, A day for people to starve their bodies? Is it bowing the head like a bulrush And lying in sackcloth and ashes? Do you call that a fast, A day when GOD is favorable?

הֲלוֹא זֶה֮ צ֣וֹם אֶבְחָרֵהוּ֒ פַּתֵּ֙חַ֙ חַרְצֻבּ֣וֹת רֶ֔שַׁע הַתֵּ֖ר אֲגֻדּ֣וֹת מוֹטָ֑ה וְשַׁלַּ֤ח רְצוּצִים֙ חׇפְשִׁ֔ים
וְכׇל־מוֹטָ֖ה תְּנַתֵּֽקוּ׃

No, this is the fast I desire: To unlock fetters of wickedness,
And untie the cords of the yoke; To let the oppressed go free;
To break off every yoke.

הֲל֨וֹא פָרֹ֤ס לָֽרָעֵב֙ לַחְמֶ֔ךָ וַעֲנִיִּ֥ים מְרוּדִ֖ים תָּ֣בִיא בָ֑יִת כִּֽי־תִרְאֶ֤ה עָרֹם֙ וְכִסִּית֔וֹ וּמִבְּשָׂרְךָ֖
לֹ֥א תִתְעַלָּֽם׃

It is to share your bread with the hungry, And to take the
wretched poor into your home; When you see the naked, to
clothe them, And not to ignore your own kin.

אָ֣ז יִבָּקַ֤ע כַּשַּׁ֙חַר֙ אוֹרֶ֔ךָ וַאֲרֻכָתְךָ֖ מְהֵרָ֣ה תִצְמָ֑ח וְהָלַ֤ךְ לְפָנֶ֙יךָ֙ צִדְקֶ֔ךָ כְּב֥וֹד יְהֹוָ֖ה יַאַסְפֶֽךָ׃

Then shall your light burst through like the dawn And
your healing spring up quickly; Your Vindicator shall
march before you, The Presence of GOD shall be your rear
guard.

אָ֤ז תִּקְרָא֙ וַיהֹוָ֣ה יַעֲנֶ֔ה תְּשַׁוַּ֖ע וְיֹאמַ֣ר הִנֵּ֑נִי אִם־תָּסִ֤יר מִתּֽוֹכְךָ֙ מוֹטָ֔ה שְׁלַ֥ח אֶצְבַּ֖ע וְדַבֶּר־
אָֽוֶן׃

Then, when you call, GOD will answer; When you cry,
[God] will say: Here I am. If you banish the yoke from your
midst, The menacing hand, and evil speech,

וְתָפֵ֤ק לָֽרָעֵב֙ נַפְשֶׁ֔ךָ וְנֶ֥פֶשׁ נַעֲנָ֖ה תַּשְׂבִּ֑יעַ וְזָרַ֤ח בַּחֹ֙שֶׁךְ֙ אוֹרֶ֔ךָ וַאֲפֵלָתְךָ֖ כַּֽצׇּהֳרָֽיִם׃

And you offer your compassion to the hungry And satisfy
the famished creature — Then shall your light shine in
darkness, And your gloom shall be like noonday.

וְנָחֲךָ יְהֹוָה תָּמִיד וְהִשְׂבִּיעַ בְּצַחְצָחוֹת נַפְשֶׁךָ וְעַצְמֹתֶיךָ יַחֲלִיץ וְהָיִיתָ כְּגַן רָוֶה וּכְמוֹצָא מַיִם אֲשֶׁר לֹא־יְכַזְּבוּ מֵימָיו:

> GOD will guide you always — Slaking your thirst in parched places and giving strength to your bones. You shall be like a watered garden, Like a spring whose waters do not fail.

The *haftarah* is a proclamation that ritual practice and moral behavior must exist hand-in-hand. The reading serves as a blueprint that maps out the requirements to complete our atonement, insisting that it cannot be achieved by merely fasting and participating in prayer. No matter how hard we concentrate on the words, beat our chests or prostrate ourselves, our davening must include an intentionality regarding how we treat others especially those less fortunate and how we conduct ourselves in the world.

The purpose of Yom Kippur is to complete the atonement of our sins. But we must not allow ourselves to be satisfied with merely showing up at services, fasting, and chanting the prayers as we pass the hours of this awesome holiday. We must not lull ourselves into thinking that this intense focus on ourselves is somehow the preferred way to be nor should it serve to exclude those around us. Indeed, disregarding others leads to a fundamentally flawed way of relating to God.

Once the day is over, we should hold the words of Isaiah's admonition in our hearts and endeavor to never hide behind personal ritual and communal responsibilities. Rather, we can lean on our Jewish values those very ones that we include in our daily prayers in the *birkhot haShachar* year-round and let them serve as a guide for each of us, toward building a better world — for ourselves, our neighbors, and for the world around us.

The Almighty's Puppy
Danielle Resh

Samson was my brother's first puppy, and my brother's bandaged fingers and the cuts marring his arms and legs was visual proof. The eager-eyed golden retriever was sweet, but boy, was he a chomper. Grass, clumps of mud, sticks, walls, wires— anything that was in front of Samson was vulnerable to being crushed between his shark-like teeth. It wasn't out of malice, or even self-defense; like a teething newborn, Samson just liked to bite. And if your hand got in the way of his mouth, well, that was just too bad for you.

It was *really* too bad for Josh, because he was running out of available skin for Samson to bite. My brother was determined to train the chomper out of Samson (who we had, by then, appropriately nicknamed "Chompers"). Samson had gotten much better than his earliest puppy days, when I refused to even get near him without the protection of long sleeves and oven mitts. But he still had a long way to go.

The routine was always the same. Samson, doing his crazy Samson thing, would be tugging on a rope toy, or laying down for his favorite belly rub, when he would snap his jaws at our hands. Immediately, Josh would stop playing with him and stand up. "No," he would scold him, then hold him gently, but firmly, by the collar. "No biting. No." Then, my brother would lead the sulking puppy over to the crate, where he would lock Samson in, as if letting him think about what he did. After a few minutes, he'd open the door, pet his puppy, and lean down to whisper in his floppy ear, "No more biting, okay?" while reminding him, "I love you. You're a good boy."

My brother was the ideal dog dad— having watched hours upon hours of training videos weeks before he even picked up

203

the puppy— and usually he performed this routine with a measure of calm and discipline that would give the most even-headed parent a run for their money. But one day, when in the midst of playing tug, Samson bit my brother and drew blood, the frustration crept in.

> "Samson! No!" he yelled. After dragging the guilty golden retriever to his crate, my brother returned to his seat and crossed his arms, cradling his bleeding forearm.
>
> "Are you seriously mad at a dog?" I laughed.
>
> "Yes," my brother responded, face tensed. "He knows not to bite."
>
> "But he's just a puppy."

My brother continued to sit there, angry, as I marveled. Sure, Samson knew he wasn't supposed to bite. But he was a puppy! He was a baby animal, he was teething, and for goodness sake, his ancestors were wolves— was it any wonder that his instincts had prevailed over his training? Besides, he didn't understand the consequences of his actions. He didn't know that when he sunk his sharp little puppy teeth down into my brother's skin, he hurt his beloved human deeply.

As soon as I really thought about it, the realization dawned on me— how similar we human beings are to my brother's erring puppy.

On Yom Kippur, we speak of *Avinu Malkeinu*, our Father, our King. Often, we focus on the *Malkeinu* part. We envision the judging King sitting in front of the Books of Life and Death, prepared to dole out whatever consequences our actions in the past year call for, justice-seeking and exact.

It's true that the traditional conception of G-d does encompass this aspect of strict-justice. But there's another element of G-d that appears before us on Yom Kippur, that appears even before the sovereignly element— and that's *Avinu,* our father.

To G-d as *Avinu*, we really are just puppies. We may know what we are and are not supposed to do— the 613 commandments are stated clearly in the Torah, written deep within our guts. But sometimes, instinct overcomes our training. We become mad, upset, deliriously happy, full of passion— and we do something we're not supposed to do.

We may know the rules— but do we always understand the consequences? If my brother's puppy knew he was hurting the person he most loves in the world when he bites him, would he do it? If we truly felt the tear ripped in the world, the pain we cause G-d, or the distance we put between ourselves and our Creator every time we do an *aveirah*— would we ever have done the sin in the first place?

Soon, my brother will take his puppy out of his crate. He'll smooth the soft fur on the top of his little head and whisper into his floppy ears, "It's okay. I still love you. Just please don't bite me again." And Samson will cuddle up to him, and Josh will cuddle back, and all will be okay. And then a few days, or even a few hours later, when Samson's teeth hurt and he's hungry or tired or full of energy, he'll bite again, because he's just a puppy. And my brother will take him to his crate and make sure he learns not to bite anyone else. And then he'll take him out and tell them that he loves him once again.

Because he's just a puppy.

Because he's *his* puppy.

And I'll turn to my prayerbook and incline my ear towards the Heavens, and try to hear the small, still voice of G-d whispering, "It's okay. I still love you. Just don't do it again."

And I'll know that even when I do, that voice will still be there, reassuring, caressing, loving unconditionally.

Because I'm His puppy.

Is Forgiveness possible without fasting? (Yom Kippur 5783)

Yael Szulanski

Six years ago, I wrote an article about fasting on Yom Kippur. I was 35 weeks pregnant with my first child, and by some miracle, felt well enough to fast. That was the last — and only-time since the age of 12, that I have been able to fast without causing cascading negative effects to my mental and physical health.

When approaching this topic again this year, I wondered whether I should focus on the structure around fasting on Yom Kippur, or on my own experience as a person in recovery (forever) from mental illness and disordered eating. I chose to do a little bit of both. I preface this by saying that I am in no way a halachic or medical authority on this topic, and anyone struggling would do best to consult professionals. I simply offer the following: a cleared out space in the dusty window that this topic can be, and my own little face peering through it.

Where does Yom Kippur come from? It comes right after the story in the Torah, where Aharon's sons are killed by God for coming into the Tent of Meeting without being summoned. God then instructs Aharon, via Moses, on how to create a yearly ritual of cleansing self, and the community. It is basically saying, you can't show up in a sacred space at all times — there are limits, boundaries, structure.

We learn these rules in Vayikra (Leviticus) 16:

וְהָיְתָה לָכֶם לְחֻקַּת עוֹלָם בַּחֹדֶשׁ הַשְּׁבִיעִי בֶּעָשׂוֹר לַחֹדֶשׁ תְּעַנּוּ אֶת־נַפְשֹׁתֵיכֶם וְכָל־
מְלָאכָה לֹא תַעֲשׂוּ הָאֶזְרָח וְהַגֵּר הַגָּר בְּתוֹכְכֶם:

And this shall be to you a law for all time: In the seventh month, on the tenth day of the month, you shall practice self-denial; and you shall do no manner of work, neither the citizen nor the alien who resides among you.

כִּי־בַיּוֹם הַזֶּה יְכַפֵּר עֲלֵיכֶם לְטַהֵר אֶתְכֶם מִכֹּל חַטֹּאתֵיכֶם לִפְנֵי יְהֹוָה תִּטְהָרוּ:

For on this day atonement shall be made for you to cleanse you of all your sins; you shall be clean before the LORD.

שַׁבַּת שַׁבָּתוֹן הִיא לָכֶם וְעִנִּיתֶם אֶת־נַפְשֹׁתֵיכֶם חֻקַּת עוֹלָם:

It shall be a sabbath of complete rest for you, and you shall practice self-denial; it is a law for all time

The Torah does not specifically tell us what "self-denial" is — in fact, in the Gemara (Yoma 74) comically asks 'does this mean that we should sit in the hot sun, or the cold all day?' It is later on, that this is clarified to include not eating as a form of self- denial.

One of the most perplexing struggles I have encountered around this topic — for myself and others — is the feeling of shame around not fasting. Let me be clear, in situations of physical, spiritual, even emotional peril- one may be exempt from fasting. These include, but are not limited to: pregnancy, physical illness, mental health challenges of all kinds, even instances of grief and bereavement. Still, the myriad of conversations I have been a part of around this topic are filled with the unspoken question:

> "Am I not good enough because I can't fast?"
> "Can I fully be forgiven if I can't fully follow the commandment to fast?"

In the piece six years ago, I wrote:

> *"In my world, everyone fasts on Yom Kippur. Even people I know who are not otherwise observant, fast on Yom Kippur. Every year since 2008, I have faced the holiday with an immense amount of shame around the fact that, again, I would not be allowed to fast. Ironically, the shame influenced my choice around how and when I ate so that I could still hide it from people who didn't know — I ate in secret, while others were asleep or at services. Even though I am blessed with a supportive network of people, I still felt ashamed. I didn't want to "burden" anyone with what I saw as my inability, again, to 'get over this.'"*

At that time, I was just starting on my journey of deeper understanding of Jewish observance, and a modern orthodox life. My perception that "everyone fasts on Yom Kippur" came from not having access to the conversations with people who don't fast, or eat according to halachic and medical guidance — and the people who guide them. While that year, I did choose to fast — and was able to — I still felt desperately alone. Yom Kippur is a day of restriction — the state of which can lead us into deeper Teshuva — repentance, forgiveness — literally returning to a state of good standing. Yet, it is also a day for communities to come together and welcome forgiveness. Still, persons tiptoeing the line of exemptions, are often left to battle this question alone.

I come back to this piece of writing every year. I have tried, over the years, to figure out what confluence of factors came together to allow for that miracle. I found myself confused at the inverted correlation between my deepening observance, and still struggling with the fast. What I have come up with is that six years ago- the miracle itself — a pregnancy after more than a decade of illness that ravaged my mind and body. It was the most powerful energy in my body, and I benefited from it, as did my Teshuva.

One of the general principles of fasting on Yom Kippur is that those who suffer from mental health challenges are generally obligated in the Yom Kippur fast, which is a Torah obligation. However, if their mental state is such that their health is compromised by fasting, they become exempt. Still, however, if they choose to fast, this is considered a spiritual value. In other words, you don't have to if you can't — but if you can, you should.

Forgive me, but I struggle to see the path to Teshuva in that statement.

In the years where I felt that I was, perhaps, healthy enough to fast, the act itself sent me into a relapse of symptoms and disordered thinking that then, depending on the year, took me anywhere from days to weeks to recalibrate. The obligation to fast became a trigger, and one that no level of wellness was strong enough to hold off.

With each year that passes, I get stronger in my recovery, and find myself battling disordered thoughts less and less often. Still — even with the tremendous work that I do to rewire my brain, heal trauma, and live with presence and awareness — these thoughts occasionally still come in.

They look like: feeling constricted by the clothes I wear, even though I've worn them without issue before; doubting whether I can actually try a dessert — even though I've tried many desserts for years; many days where my meals look identical — just so I don't have to think about it. They also look like: spending too much time looking at parts of my body in the mirror; feeling overwhelmed for no tangible reason, other than my brain is firing on an old circuit; and still — that longing to fill the lacuna within me — the one that will never be filled.

> Yet, I wonder now, as I have every year — is teshuva possible without fasting?
> Am I betraying God by not fully restricting?
> Can I forgive myself when I have struggled to survive every year for 20 years?

Regardless of whether I fast or not, I cry every Yom Kippur in services — namely, at the recitation of God's 13 attributes of mercy. My tears fall in a mixture of gratitude and a plea — almost a begging — that this year, I can finally live free of fear, shame, and re-emerging trauma.

The 13 Attributes of Mercy are based on two verses in Exodus:

> "The Lord! The Lord! God, Compassionate and Gracious, Slow to anger and Abundant in Kindness and Truth, Preserver of kindness for thousands of generations, Forgiver of iniquity, willful sin, and error, and Who Cleanses (but does not cleanse completely, recalling the iniquity of parents upon children and grandchildren, to the third and fourth generations)" (Exodus 34:6–7).

Something about there being a divine, higher power that can help guide towards forgiveness — no matter what — uplifts me from a place of doubt, shame, and confusion. In that brief moment, when we read this — I get it. Yes, I can find Teshuva even if I don't fast. That moment is usually very brief; when I return to my thoughts on life — it all seeps back in: the fear, the doubt, the shame, the distorted image of self. I know this to be true for many who struggle with mental illness, and especially on this day.

Every year, I look at different Rabbinic responsa around the question of someone with a history of eating disorders needing

211

to fast on Yom Kippur. While many of my own personal spiritual guides have told me, "no, if you even feel that you are in danger — the answer is no" or even "A person with a history of eating disorders should never fast — they are considered in constant peril." Even with "permission," I still find myself doubting, questioning, and wondering If I need to keep things a secret. It is a schism between the part of me that has always wanted to "just be normal" and the part of me that has come to peace, put in years of work for recovery, grieved years and relationships lost to illness, and now finds gratitude in the smallest moments.

Mental illness does not need to "look" a certain way. One can appear fully functional, happy, healthy — and in reality, be far from it. In preparing to write this piece, I revisited old journals I've kept at different stages of recovery. A recurring theme in them is: being told that I am doing well, when internally I am crumbling. Some are from not too long ago.

The crux of the issue is: dissonance. Our outside lived experience of this day — and of life in general — is in huge contradiction to our internal world. Why must we pretend that we are fasting? Why do we say that we are okay when we aren't? Why do we need this to be just like everyone else for us, when it isn't? I take a deep breath during the reading of the 13 attributes of mercy, but then I hold it in until the day is done.

I propose, as we prepare for this day, that if we are not fasting for whatever reason — or even if we need to make adjustments to our practice — that we focus on easing that dissonance. Even if we are fasting, and we feel like we need to adjust during the day — that dissonance can exist. Forgiveness can seep into the tiniest cracks and expand to heal scars with golden edges. It can fill voids with warmth, and it can release tension — even decades old.

The struggle on Yom Kippur, to find reconciliation within our own selves, with our loved ones, with God is hard enough, let us not make it harder by punishing ourselves for taking care of ourselves. If you can fast — great. If you can't — also great.

Actually, really, and truly. If we see this love of self as a divine act, then it is not an issue of "it would be preferable if you fasted, but we get why you don't." It becomes "we support you putting your continued existence as a priority and welcome you into the community as you are." This is how it should be, and this is how I choose to see it this year. I offer myself as a welcoming space for anyone who is struggling with this day. You do not need to hold shame, and you do not need to keep your self-care a secret.

There is no shame in showing yourself love, in choosing another path. Spiritual fulfillment need not come from the letter of the law, but rather from enough structure so that spirit can be upheld with strength and dignity. Spiritually, we can all soar when we allow ourselves to be as we are, without judgment, and without fear. We are welcomed to the community as we are, atone as we are, and forgiven as we are. In fact, keeping yourself alive and whole — mentally, physically, emotionally, spiritually — is a mitzvah greater than all, even on Yom Kippur.

Sukkot/ Simchat Torah

Ushpizin/Ushpizot
Esther in the Sukkah

Naomi Bromberg Bar-Yam, Ph.D.

Over the last few decades, the custom of inviting *ushpizot*, women from our tradition, into the sukkah along with the men of *ushpizin*, has grown and expanded. As we welcome Esther, we think about her connection to *sukkot* and the *sukkah*.

I am honored to be invited into your sukkah to share with you this joyous and inspiring holiday. My name and my story give me a special connection to Sukkot. You know me as Esther, "hidden one," niece of Mordecai, wife of Ahasuerus, queen of Persia, savior of the Jewish people. I am also Hadassah, myrtle, one of the *arba'at haminim*. These *minim* have been compared to the four kinds of Jews who, together, make up our people. Despite my royalty and my unique place in Jewish history, I am, like you, one of our people; without each of us, we are incomplete. The *hadas* also symbolizes success and immortality; because of its fragrant oils *hadassim* grow in drought, they quickly resprout after fire and their branches remain upright and fresh long after cutting them. With the help of God and my uncle Mordecai, I too was successful in helping our people survive the crisis that almost destroyed us. I am also Esther, the hidden one. There is much hiding, deceit and secrecy in my story; Vashti hid herself, Haman deceived Ahasuerus about his evil intentions, Bigtana and Teresh secretly plotted against my husband, and I hid from him my full identity.

My names reveal the struggles and paradoxes of my story and, indeed, of our national story. I am Hadassah, strong, upright, flourishing in prosperity and in hardship. I am Esther, hidden, full of secrets and yet, the delicate fragrance of Hadassah is impossible for Esther to hide completely.

The sukkah, where you sit now, is a symbol of our vulnerability in the face of natural and human forces. Its shaky beams, flapping walls, open branched roof, expose us to the wind and rain, which we need to live, and from which we need the protection of secure roof and walls. In the urban settings where you and I live, the sukkah is also public. Like the fragrance of the *hadas,* one cannot erect and dwell in a sukkah and hide one's identity.

Like Joseph, another honored guest in your sukkah, and like many of you, my story takes place outside of Israel, among other nations. Joseph and Mordecai recognized God's hand in our rises to power, so that we could save our brethren. Throughout our history, continuing today, many of us have achieved power and influence in our respective governments and fields, blessing us with the opportunity and responsibility to help our people survive, grow and thrive.

It has been a pleasure to join you in the sukkah, this public place of vulnerability and strength, joy and introspection. Here, Esther emerges, no longer needing to hide in self-protection. Here, I am Hadassah, one member of the nation of Israel, from whom I draw strength, and to whom I contribute what protection and wisdom I can.

I look forward to meeting you again in a few months, amid the frolicking of Purim and next year in the sukkah, our season of quieter joy.

A New Prayer for Rain 5784/2023

Ronitte Friedman and Odeni Sheer

A few years ago, when the silence of women's voices in public ritual became deafening, I made a rash promise: to right/write the wrong when I could.

My quest begins with *T'fillat Geshem*, a Top Ten prayer in terms of its status. Geshem? Top Ten? On first glance it feels like an unexpected choice, but we have three signals that unequivocally point to its importance. Firstly, it's a true "OG"- it's one of the prayers in the very first siddurim, composed during the Gaonic period which ran from the end of the 6th century to the middle of the 11th. Now note its prime time location in the davening, right at the beginning of the chazzan's repetition of *Musaf*. Finally, the *Aron Kodesh* is opened. All of these signal that this is a major prayer. So it's a fair question to ask: why rain?

The simplest reason is the physical one. In the agrarian world of 6th century Israel rain means life, and a good rainy season was so critical that it merited a unique prayer recited with all possible pomp and circumstance. On a metaphysical level, rain is a metaphor for our tricky relationship with God. No rain, no crops, so pray for rain. Too much rain, no crops, so pray for the rain to stop. We can't control or command rain. No weather app can evoke it. We rely on God for rain. All we can do is pray, a humbling fact for us 21st century high tech big shots. Now I understand why *T'fillat Geshem* is a major prayer.

But *T'fillat Geshem* has no women, and frankly, some of the connections of the highlighted men to water, don't hold water.

As the prayer was composed 1500 years ago, we are neither surprised nor upset at this absence of women. It's time to write women into Geshem. Which women should I include? What should the inclusion/exclusion criteria be?

I dared to envision a brand new genre, highlighting the vast contributions of women to Judaism. I decided that to be considered for my *Geshem*, a woman had to meet 4 strict criteria:

1. the woman's relationship with water had to be significant enough that in her merit we can pray for, and expect rain.
2. the woman's actions had to create a plot shift in the narrative- there needed to be a clear before and after.
3. the woman needed to be important enough that we know her by name.
4. the woman must appear in the Tanach, making her story foundational for us.

The criteria led me to four women. Each one of these women had a unique and completely different relationship with God. Each story highlights a different angle of our relationship with God. The women are Hagar, Rivka, Miriam and Bat Sheva. Unexpectedly I noticed that each one correlated to a man celebrated in Geshem: Hagar/Avraham, Rivka/Yitzchak, Miriam/Moshe, Bat Sheva/David.

Time to compose. Should I follow the normal convention of our tfilot and present these heroines in chronological order: Hagar, Rivka, Miriam, Bat Sheva? Or should the poem reflect how synonymous this character is with water? Miriam, Miriam, Miriam, Miriam.

Next: Language. Do I write in Hebrew? Biblical or modern? Or Aramaic, the lingua franca. I settled on the 21st century vernacular of English. And still, I was stuck. I'm a writer and I like to think I'm a good one but my relationship with these women didn't feel like it could be expressed in a tfila or in a piyut. So I wrote a spoken word poem, a transcript of the direct conversations this 21st century woman had with these biblical heroes. When I think of *Geshem*, I think of them.

Hagar

You strayed
got lost
desert all around
desert thorns inside your soul
tossed your boy in scrubby brush
you couldn't bear his parched cries
you ran
but not too far
you cried to God
throat clogged with sand
voice breaking
your tears
the only water in the arid
desert
you trusted the angel
you were so thirsty
what was
one more leap
of faith
the angel said
take your son's hand
He Will Be a Great Nation
you believed
then God opened your eyes
And there was water

Rivka

You saw a stranger at the well
you just a young girl
your faith so pure
your purity unsullied
your water jug no
protection from harm
you talked to him
you did not run away
as young girls are taught
you drew water for the stranger
you drew water for his camels
your actions were kindness
did your innocence protect you
did you ever feel unsafe
were you terrified when he placed a
gold nose ring upon your face
did you feel trapped by
gold bangles encircling your arm
still you took him home
don't you think that's too much
your kindness was authentic
your destiny was now declared
You would be a matriarch of our nation

Miriam

Lemme get this straight
you put your
3 month old
baby brother in a
what's that
I can't hear you

222

a wicker basket
a wicker basket
do you hear me now
but don't worry mom
I made it
waterproof
with clay and tar
I think it will hold
you placed him in this
dubious basket
you put him in the River Nile
you set him down in river reeds
you hid yourself
now all you could do was
wait and watch
were you fierce and hopeful
were you desperate and broken
were you all of that
then Pharoah's daughter
picked him up
and the rest
as they say
is history
But seriously

Bat Sheva

You took a bath
you made yourself pure
you thought you were safe
but he saw you
you were seen
talk about violation of privacy
you were beautiful

he took you didn't ask
there was no consent
you were pregnant
you sent word
he dispatched your husband
to die in combat
there was no conversation
then he took you as his wife
did you love him?
**Did you know you would be the
mother of kings?**

Our Beautiful Elders
(Ha'azinu)
Rabbanit Bracha Jaffe

Parashat Ha'azinu is written in poetic format, with short and pithy phrases that are oft-quoted. The poem contains lessons that Moshe wishes to gift to the Jewish nation, many of which address the continuity of our legacy and passing wisdom from generation to generation.

Many of the verses are written using poetic parallelism where the second half of a phrase mirrors the first half. A perfect example of this is [Deut 32:9]:

זְכֹר יְמוֹת עוֹלָם, בִּינוּ שְׁנוֹת דֹּר-וָדֹר

"Remember the days of old ⇔ Consider the years of many generations;

And the verse continues:

שְׁאַל אָבִיךָ וְיַגֵּדְךָ, זְקֵנֶיךָ וְיֹאמְרוּ לָךְ.

Ask your father, and he will tell you ⇔ Your elders, and they will answer you."

Here is a deeper and more poignant way to understand the second half of this verse:

שְׁאַל אָבִיךָ וְיַגֵּדְךָ: "Ask your father and **he** will tell you"

What will he tell you? He will say:

זְקֵנֶיךָ וְיֹאמְרוּ לָךְ: "[Go to] your elders; [from an earlier generation], and **they** will answer you."

It can be natural to turn to our own parents for counsel and advice. Here, the parents are reminding their children who **they** turn to for advice, as well as how much wisdom there is to be gleaned from those who have greater life experience.

As we approach the holiday of Sukkot, there is another beautiful parallelism that brings home the same thought. In *Sefer VaYikra* we are commanded to take the *arba minim*, the Four Species [Lev 23:40]: וּלְקַחְתֶּם לָכֶם בַּיּוֹם הָרִאשׁוֹן פְּרִי עֵץ הָדָר - You shall take for yourself on the first day [of Sukkot] the fruit of *etz hadar* - majestic trees" which is the *etrog*. There are many people who spend a lot of time, every year, searching for the most beautiful, the most perfect *etrog*.

But did you know that the exact same word *Hadar* is used for describing how we should honor and adorn our elders? In *Parashat Kedoshim* it says [Lev 19:32]

מִפְּנֵי שֵׂיבָה תָּקוּם, וְהָדַרְתָּ פְּנֵי זָקֵן
"You shall rise before the elderly person, the one with white hair, *vehadarta*, and you shall exalt the countenance of the elder."

As our verse in *Ha'azinu* suggests:

"Ask your father and **he** will tell you, Go to your elders; and **they** will answer you."

Consider - how treasured and precious our older generations will feel when we ask them to share their thoughts and wisdom with us.

Chag Same'ach!

Sukkot: Teshuva Redux

Chaye Kohl

> *Va'yis'u meiSukkot:*
> And they journeyed from Sukkot
> (*Shemot* 13:20).

> *Ba'Sukkot teshvu shivat yomim:*
> You shall dwell in Sukkot seven days
> (*Vayikra* 23:42).

A conundrum presented in two verses - for lay readers and Biblical commentators. Is Sukkot a place? Yes. Is Sukkot a holiday? Yes! Is there a mitzvah to journey back to this place called Sukkot to commemorate the holiday? No.

And if we use the "You shall dwell in booths (Sukkot)" as a directive to commemorate the leaving of Egypt and dwelling under the protection of G-d in the desert – then shouldn't Sukkot the holiday come soon after Pesach?

You may have the same questions. You may have heard this Dvar Torah before. Mostly, for me, these questions cause me to focus on some things that have been on my mind since the beginning of the month of Elul: New Year's resolutions.

Chachamim have debated the question about why we celebrate Sukkot during the month of Tishrei. If we sit in Sukkot/ Booths to commemorate how the Israelites lived in the desert after *Yetziat Mitzrayim*, logically we should be celebrating in

228

Nisan, the month during which the Exodus from Egypt took place. Perhaps we should be having Seder in the Sukkah?

In most countries, Tishrei, coming in the beginning of the Fall season, is not the time of year when people would ordinarily spend long periods of time chatting and eating outdoors. So, our sitting in the Sukkah is clearly being done because it is a mitzvah from Hashem, not a recreational choice.

Chag HaSukkot, also known as *Chag Ha'aseef*, is the time when gathering the harvest is over, and the silos are full.

Agriculturally flush, a person might say: *Kochi v'otzem yadi asu li et hachayil hazeh*: my own efforts brought me all these wonderful things. When we follow Hashem's commandment to sit in the Sukkah, it reminds us that indeed all our bounty is from G-d.

Which brings me to New Year's resolutions. All during this holiday season I have been thinking about what G-d really wants from me.

Six weeks before Sukkot, when the month of Elul began, we began the process of intense soul searching. Chances are we all made some sort of decisions to change behaviors that we were not happy with. Perhaps we decided to take better care of ourselves through diet and exercise (*u'shmartem et nafshosechem meod, meod*). Or we resolved to be better and more understanding friends (*v'ahavta l'ray'acha kamocha*). Or we determined to be better children/ brothers / sisters (*kabed et avicha v'et emecha*). ˅

So... How are you doing with your resolutions? Feeling successful? Feeling less than happy with your results? Elul began weeks ago. Yom Kippur was less than a week ago. How are you doing with those resolutions to change? Are you feeling some discomfort about your progress during this Sukkot holiday?

Research on habit breaking and making indicates that it takes at least 30 days to break a habit, and 30 – 60 days to cultivate a good habit. Scott Young and James Clear both write about the stages of habit breaking and habit making.

According to these experts, bad habits are often a way of dealing with stress and boredom. It is up to us to develop new and healthy ways to deal with stress and boredom. Recognizing the causes of our bad habits helps us begin to overcome them.

According to these experts on habitual behavior, the best way to eliminate a bad habit is to replace it with a good habit – a healthy type of behavior. We are urged to choose a substitute and avoid things that will trigger a bad habit. James Clear says: "Your environment makes your bad habit easier and good habits harder. Change your environment and you can change the outcome."

Those who wish to change their behaviors are each urged to find a "chevruta" and surround themselves with people who live the way they want to live. And it is important to see ourselves as succeeding. And we need to recognize that we may fail – but we have the power to get back on track.

Sukkot are places where we can sit with people who love us; those who are living a lifestyle we want to live. When we sit in the Sukkah – not in the comfort of our dining and living rooms - we are remembering the early days of a new nation, fresh from slavery, who needed to break the habits of servitude to human masters and create a spiritual life where they could serve the Master of the Universe. The *Bnei Yisrael* slipped sometimes; the *Chumash* chronicles their complaining, their overt sinning, and their contrition. Jewish history is rife with these stories of mistakes and renewal.

Sukkot is a time for us to show our commitment to G-d and to spend time with our family and friends. Now, as the season of *Chagim* draws to a close, let us re-examine how we started back in Elul. We should make the adjustments that are needed, and look forward to a year of health and joy. *Chag Sameach!*

Insights Into the Etrog

Sharona Halickman

In Vayikra, Emor 23:40, we are told "You shall take for yourselves pri etz hadar- the fruit of the beautiful tree."

How do we know that this fruit is the etrog? According to Ramban, the word etrog is the Aramaic word for the Hebrew word hadar. The word etrog means desirable, Onkelos says that it is nechmad, pleasant to the sight.

According to the Kabbala, pri etz hadar is the fruit in which there is a great deal of desire. This is the fruit that Adam and Chava sinned with in Breisheet 3:6: "And the woman perceived that the tree was good for eating and that it was a delight to the eyes and that the tree was desirable as a means of wisdom and she took of the fruit and she ate".

Chava's punishment for eating the fruit was that she would have a difficult time during childbirth.

How do we make a tikkun, correction for Chava's eating of the fruit without permission?

There is a custom for a pregnant woman to bite off the end of the etrog (pitom)on Hoshana Raba. According to Chava Weissler in Voices of the Matriarchs, this custom was thought to ensure an easy childbirth. The custom appears both in Tsenerene (a women's bible published in 1600) as well as in books of tkines (women's prayers).

After biting off the pitom, the pregnant woman should give tzedakah, pray that she has an easy labor and recite the following prayer:

> "Ribono shel olam, because Chava ate of the etrog, all of us women must suffer such great pangs as to die. Had I been there, I would not have had any enjoyment from the fruit. Just as now I have not wanted to render the etrog unfit during the whole seven days when it was used for a mitzvah. Now on Hoshana Raba the mitzvah is no longer applicable, but I am still not in a hurry to eat it..."

I am not guaranteeing that this custom will make childbirth a breeze, but it certainly can't hurt.

The Gemara in Ketubot 61a adds that a pregnant woman who actually eats the etrog (after the holiday) will have children that smell good.

Bon Appetit!

The Journey of the Arava
Rabbanit Bracha Jaffe

How many of you used to read K'Tonton when you were young? Or maybe you read it now to your children or to your grandchildren. K'tonton - meaning very little - like *katan katan* is about a very little boy, no bigger than a thumb who loves everything Jewish. K'tonton may start out small but by the end of each adventure and story - he has grown greatly in stature and standing.

On Sukkot we have a similar story. Allow me to take you on a journey - the journey of the willow - the Aravah.

We start out Sukkot with 4 species that are bundled together:

- The beautiful *Etrog*: with delightful fragrance and pleasant taste.
- The majestic *Lulav*: with no fragrance but with the sweet taste of its fruit - the date
- The fragrant *Hadas*: with no taste but with aromatic scent
- And the lowly *Aravah* - with no taste and no fragrance.

The Aravah seems to be the least sturdy of the *arba'at haminim* as it dries out so quickly. We have all experienced Aravah-phobia: are my Aravot dried up or are they still kosher to use on the 5th day? The 6th day? By Hoshana Rabba - forget it! These four species are bundled together, lifted and waved in six directions. The Mishnah in Masechet Sukkah is unusually verbose, going into great detail about how to bundle and tie them together and about when and where they are lifted and waved.

The Mishnah then goes on to describe how on each day of the festival, the people would encircle the מזבח - the altar - once. On the last day of Sukkot, Hoshanah Rabbah, they would encircle the altar seven times. Then the *Mizbe'ach* would be draped with ערבות - willows - and the people would exclaim: "יופי לך מזבח – **How beautiful you look O altar.**"

This feels extraordinary! The one species which has no outstanding attributes - no special characteristics - is the one chosen to beautify and grace the מזבח at the culmination of the Sukkot festival. This מין went from the lowest of the low to the highest of the high. How did this happen?

I have another question as well: The Midrash in Vayikra Rabba compares the ארבעת המינים to four types of Jews: those with Torah learning and mitzvot, those with no learning but with mitzvot, those with mitzvot but no Torah learning and those - like the Aravah - with no Torah learning and no mitzvot.

The Midrash then continues:

ומה הקב"ה עושה להם?

What does God do with these four types of Jews?

לאבדן אי אפשר

God cannot destroy them!

אלא אמר הקדוש ברוך הוא

Rather God says:

יוקשרו כולם אגודה אחת והן מכפרין אלו על אלו

235

The four species shall be tied together in one bundle, and they shall each atone for each other.

I can see how the other three species who each have at least Torah learning or mitzvot could help atone for the others. But what can the poor Aravah do with nothing in his (or her) pocket to offer for atonement?

As we answer these questions, we will gain some marvelous insights into community and how these reverberate through the themes of Sukkot and its mitzvot.

Let me address the second question first - what does the Aravah have to offer to atone for the other species' wrongdoings?

VaYikrah Rabba (30:14) describes the **ד' מינים** this way:

1. The *Etrog* represents the heart
2. The *Hadas* has leaves shaped like an eye
3. The *Lulav* represents the spine
4. The *Aravah* represents the lips

And in fact - the leaves of the Aravah **are** shaped like lips - even down to the line in the middle! The Sefer HaChinuch explains that the *Aravah* reminds us to be careful of what we say while others understand it as an invitation to prayer. I would suggest that the lips of the *Aravah* remind us that everyone has what to offer the other and that would be - a **SMILE**. Perhaps this is exactly how the *Aravah* helps the other species (or types of Jews) atone for their sins - by creating warmth and peace between people.

In fact, though there are very few Halachot associated with the *Aravot*, one of them speaks to exactly this idea. The leaves of the *Aravah* may not be like a מסור - a saw. The edges of the Aravah must be smooth - and not jagged like the teeth of a saw. A saw is used to cut something into pieces - exactly the opposite of the curved lips of the *Aravah* which can bond and bring others together.

Rabbi Efraim Mirvis, chief rabbi of England, points out that the very name *Aravah* in Hebrew, means "mixed". Perhaps that is where the *Aravah* draws its strength - by giving to others and receiving from others. The *Aravah* does not have inherent beauty on its own and it does not stand on its own. It is literally cradled and carried in a little basket - papoose-style - together with the *Hadasim* and the *Lulav*.

This then is the essence of our answer to the first question - How the *Aravah* journeys from being a seemingly minor and insignificant player to surpassing all the others in its ability to adorn and beautify the *mizbe'ach*. It is through being bound and held together with the other species that the *Aravah* attains this stature and presence which it does not have when it starts out on its own.

We learn this lesson directly from God as the One who cradles and holds us in our Sukkot. Rabbi Eliezer in Masechet Sukkah describes the Sukkot as ענני הכבוד - the Clouds of Glory. I imagine Bnei Yisrael wrapped and cocooned in soft white clouds, shielded from the sun and the cold, from the wind and dust. Carried and nestled in God's hands.

237

מה הקדוש ברוך הוא נקרא רחום, אף אתה היה רחום; מה הקדוש ברוך הוא
נקרא חנון, אף אתה היה חנון;

"As God is merciful so must we be merciful, as God is
compassionate, so must we be compassionate."

There is a great lesson to be learned here for our communities.
There are those who have so much to give and yet may never
have an opportunity to excel. For the willow to succeed - the
community must cradle and carry those who stand out with
their fragrance and pleasant taste as well as those who may not
seem to have what to offer.

Let me share a story that happened in our community. A
woman came to shul to say kaddish. Her cousin was not well
and couldn't make it to shul. She asked for her to say kaddish
for her mother's yahrtzeit. This little act brought comfort and
solace to them both and - I believe - elevated her mother's
neshamah.

And - through the power of the community, people are
brought to serve on committees, to be involved in synagogue
initiatives, to take on responsibility for communal projects.

As a result, we have people succeeding in spectacular fashion
and that is what we learn from the willow. What starts out
being ordinary becomes extraordinary. What starts out, at the
beginning of the festival of Sukkot, being totally eclipsed by
the other species, becomes, by the end of the festival, the
greatest of them all.

But there is more: it is not only those people who are often
quietly in the background that we must cradle and hold. Many

if not all of us have been in those places at different times in our lives.

Sometimes we may feel like the *Etrog*: with fragrance and taste, with much to offer others, rich in experience and skills to enhance the world around us.

Other times we may feel like the *Lulav* or the *Hadas*, with perhaps less to offer but still substantial and meaningful.

And other times when we may feel empty or bereft of something to give, in the shadows. The lesson of the *Aravah* is two-fold: for the community and for each one of us. As individuals we hear that we always carry beauty within us, that we can always find something to give the other - starting from a smile, a hug or a listening ear.

As a community we are entrusted with the care of each and every person - to hold them close and lift them, cherish them and help them feel special.

The journey of the Aravah is about to come to a close. This evening begins the festival of Hoshanah Rabbah and the *Aravot* will complete their passage from unremarkable to remarkable, from unexceptional to beautiful.

So do not be sad when the leaves of your *Aravot* dry up. Be of good cheer that they teach us a message year after year; they do their service and beautify themselves along the way.
Mo'adim LeSimchah v'Chag Same'ach!

On Permanence and Impermanence: Reflections on the Sukkah

Rabbi Dr. Erin Leib Smokler

(previously published on Jofa.org)

The holiday of Sukkot is famously one of joy.

The Torah exhorts us "בחגך ושמחת," "You shall rejoice in your festival" (Deuteronomy 16:14). It then follows with an even more bold demand: "שמח אך והיית" — "You shall have nothing but joy" (Deut. 16:15). Our liturgy accordingly refers to the holiday as שמחתינו זמן, the time of our joy. This repetitive, all-encompassing language raises the question: What about Sukkot makes it so uniquely joyous? And just what kind of *simha* are we after? A close look at the central symbol of the holiday, the *sukkah*, yields some insight. The foundational command for the *sukkah* is found in Leviticus 23:42-43:

בסכת תשבו שבעת ימים כל האזרח בישראל ישבו בסכת מב.
הושבתי את בני ישראל בהוציאי אותם מארץ מג למען ידעו דרתיכם כי בסכות
מצרים אני ה אלוקיכם.

(42) You shall live in booths for seven days; all citizens in Israel should live in booths, (43) in order that future generations may know that I made the Israelite people live in booths when I brought them out of the land of Egypt, I the Lord your God.

240

Clarifying these verses, the Talmud explains:

וְרָבָא אָמַר ,מֵהָכָא :"בַּסּוּכּוֹת תֵּשְׁבוּ שִׁבְעַת יָמִים"
אָמְרָה תּוֹרָה :כָּל שִׁבְעַת הַיָּמִים צֵא מִדִּירַת קֶבַע וְשֵׁב בְּדִירַת עֲרַאי
And Rava said, "From the passage, 'You shall live in booths seven days' (Lev. 23:42), the Law commanded that, for all seven days, you shall leave your permanent dwelling and live in a temporary dwelling." (Tractate Sukkah 2a)

The *mitzvah* of *sukkah* is here distilled to its essence: The *sukkah* is a place of impermanence. As we will see, it is a space that is unstable, unrooted, and insufficiently protective. It is ephemeral and fragile, leafy and leaky. In every sense, it is *not home*.

The halakha cements this insistence on impermanence and instability in both time and space. The first chapters of Mishnah Sukkah illustrate this well. A *sukkah* must be temporal, we are told, made exclusively for use on the holiday (Mishnah Sukkah 1:1). It must be humble and unmistakable for a home. It therefore cannot be taller than 20 cubits (1:1). It cannot be built within a house or beneath a tree (1:2). Inside of it, one cannot sleep beneath a bed (2:1) nor eat beneath a sheet (1:3). In other words, the *sukkah* itself must be exposed to the elements and one must be exposed to them while in it.

Augmenting this theme of exposure is the סכך, the flimsy roof of the *sukkah* that must provide shade but not cover. The סכך must be made of organic matter, grown from the ground, but no longer attached to it (1:4). It cannot be bundled or too wide (1:5-7). That is, it cannot shelter too much. It must leave room to see sky and stars, and thus to endure rain and wind.

In sum, the *sukkah* — the "עראי דירת, "the dwelling that is no home — must be a vulnerable structure that also generates an

241

experience of vulnerability. One must be ever conscious of impermanence while in its midst.

On *Sukkot*, Rava said "צא מדירת קבע ושב בדירת עראי," one must exit the known world of security, of קבע, and enter a world of insecurity.

***

And yet, a shocking paradox awaits us at the end of chapter two of the Mishnah. Having established unequivocally the importance of impermanence, an audacious demand is issued:

> כל שבעת ימים אדם עושה סוכתו קבע וביתו עראי.
>
> All seven days, one must make one's *sukkah* permanent and one's home impermanent. (Mishnah Sukkah 2:9)

That which is quintessentially קבע — home — must be rendered עראי on Sukkot. And that which is quintessentially עראי — the *sukkah* — must be rendered קבע! That very structure that embodies and engenders the ephemeral is somehow to be given roots. That meek place of exposure is to be embraced as a reliable shelter. One must find a way to transform impermanence into permanence.

How? The Gemara explains:

> הָיוּ לוֹ כֵּלִים נָאִים מַעֲלָן לַסּוּכָּה ,מַצָּעוֹת נָאוֹת — מַעֲלָן לַסּוּכָּה ,אוֹכֵל וְשׁוֹתֶה וּמְטַיֵּיל בַּסּוּכָה .מְנָא הָנֵי מִילֵּי ?דְּתָנוּ רַבָּנַן :"תֵּשְׁבוּ" — כְּעֵין תָּדוּרוּ
>
> If one has fine utensils, bring them into the *sukkah*. If one has fine bedding, transfer it to the *sukkah*. And one should eat, drink, and walk in the *sukkah*. Whence is this deduced? From what the rabbis taught: "You shall *live* [in booths seven days" (Lev. 23:42)] — [Live] as you normally do. (Tractate Sukkah 28b)

242

To establish the *sukkah* as a home, one must act as if it is one.

***

What are we to make of this play between the transient and the intransient? Why would the rabbis go to such lengths to construct a flimsy edifice only to undermine it? What is the meaning of a life lived self-consciously 'as if'? Herein lies the deep message of the *sukkah*, and the source of its *simha*. It is nothing less than a lesson in how to live with integrity in a fragile, uncertain world. At the start of a new year, the *sukkah* offers habituation into a life lived with eyes wide open.

After Rosh Hashana and Yom Kippur, with all of their confident declarations — about who God is and who we are, about the justice of the world and the pathways to forgiveness — Sukkot comes to destabilize us. Conviction is surely a great religious value, but certainty is a grave religious danger. At best, it breeds complacence; at worst, hubristic fundamentalism and intolerance. Certainty blinds the mind and locks the spirit. So in a move of dizzying contrast, Sukkot provides an antidote. It comes to remind us that God cannot be fully known, that the ways of the world cannot be fully comprehended, that our own selves cannot be fully pinned down. For existence is fundamentally unpredictable and unstable, or "הבלים הבל", "as Kohelet says, "utterly evanescent" (Ecclesiastes 1:2). The universe is always changing and we are ever in flux, sometimes birthing, sometimes dying; sometimes building, sometimes coming apart (Ecc. 3:2-3).

When we enter a *sukkah* of instability — where walls are not solid, where we lack a roof over our heads — we are forced to confront our radical exposure. We must acknowledge that we exist in inescapable uncertainty. We must see that we cannot, ultimately, be sheltered. In this experience of raw vulnerability, we are stripped of illusions of permanence and are thrown into consciousness of impermanence. The world, alas, is unmistakably a עראי דירת.

How, then, are we to live? What are we to do with this awareness of הבל? The *sukkah* offers a profound answer: "תדורו כעין תשבו." Learn to dwell inside of those fragile places. Make of them a קבע דירת. Act as if you are here to stay. Insist on the wild possibility of building, even on shifty soil. Assert the capacity to make enduring commitments, even in the absence of certainties. Set up a home and beautify it. Invite *ushpizin*, guests, into it. Create relationships and nourish them. Bring your finest self and your finest stuff into the space that you set up. Feed yourself and those around you. Love with abandon. Invest in a future. Dare to bring new life into this crazy world. And when it rains, offer shelter where you can, knowing all too well that you cannot shield. These are the modest requests of a faithful life.

In the words of Rabbi Jonathan Sacks: Jewish faith is not a metaphysical wager, a leap into the improbable. It is the courage to see the world as it really is, without the comfort of myth or the self-pity of despair...[1]

Jewish faith is not about believing the world to be other than it is. It is not about ignoring the evil, the darkness, and the pain. It is about the courage, endurance, and the capacity to hold fast to ideals even when they are ignored by others. It is the ability to see the world for what it is and yet still believe that it could be different. It is about not giving up, not letting go. Faith is what the Song of Songs calls "the love which is stronger than death" (Song of Songs 8:6).[2]

Indeed, the challenge of faith, as issued by the *sukkah*, mirrors the challenge of love. It calls forth from us the audacity to bind ourselves in perpetuity to that which can never be fully known and to put down roots in spite of all the risk. And what a deep joy that can be!

The *simha* of Sukkot is thus to be found here, in the enlivening choice to confront the uncertainty of existence head on and to live boldly and beautifully in the face of it. In actively transforming impermanence into permanence, a עראי דירת into a קבע דירת, the frail *sukkah* of the world becomes a joyful home indeed.

Hag sameah!

Notes:
1. Jonathan Sacks, *Radical Then, Radical Now* (London, Continuum, 2003), p. 214
2. Ibid, p. 182

Erin Leib Smokler is pursuing a PhD in Philosophy and Religion at the University of Chicago's Committee on Social Thought. She teaches Jewish Philosophy at the Drisha Institute for Jewish Education and holds an MA from the University of Chicago and a BA from Harvard University. Her writing has appeared in The New Republic, The New York Times Book Review, The Jerusalem Report, and The New York Jewish Week.

From Goads to Girls' Ball Games: Midrash and Kohelet 12:11

Anna Urowitz-Freudenstein, PhD
Toronto, Ontario, Canada

One of the most difficult books of the bible to understand is Kohelet, or Ecclesiastes, which is traditionally read on the Shabbat of Sukkot. In addition to the difficult, often pessimistic philosophical concepts in it, there are also challenging words and phrases. The latter are often addressed by rabbinic commentaries in order to provide clarity and to find more meaning in them. One of the difficult verses (12:11) begins:

דִּבְרֵי חֲכָמִים כַּדָּרְבֹנוֹת...

The words of the wise are as goads...

For those of us who do not keep flocks of animals in our yards, one of the first questions about this verse might be 'what is a goad?'. (It is a spiked stick used to drive cattle.) This might be quickly followed by the question 'why are the words of the wise compared to pointy sticks?'.

Avoiding such a negative comparison with a potential lethal weapon the rabbis of the midrash (Tanchuma, Beha'alotcha 15:1) propose a paronomasic* interpretation of the unusual plural Hebrew noun by splitting it into two words - כדורבנות / כדור בנות - which transforms goads into "girls' ball[game]".

The midrash explains that the "words of the wise", that is the Torah, were passed to the Jewish people at Mt. Sinai from Hashem, just as girls pass a ball from one to another as they play. Presumably these words of Torah wisdom also are expected to be continued to be passed, from generation to generation, from teacher to student, from parent to child, in a careful, purposeful, and joyous manner.

*paronomasia
noun (Rhetoric)

1. the use of a word in different senses or the use of words similar in sound to achieve a specific effect, as humor or a dual meaning; punning.
2. a pun.

Revelations About Circles and Cyclical Dances on Simchat Torah

Shoshanah Weiss

In the book of Shmot parshat Beshalach Chapter 15/20-the posuk from the Torah says:

וַתִּקַּח מִרְיָם הַנְּבִיאָה אֲחוֹת אַהֲרֹן אֶת־הַתֹּף בְּיָדָהּ
וַתֵּצֶאןָ כָל־הַנָּשִׁים אַחֲרֶיהָ בְּתֻפִּים וּבִמְחֹלֹת:

Then Miriam the prophetess, Aaron's sister, picked up a hand-drum, and all the women went out after her in dance with hand-drums.

The tof is a drum. Rashi writes that women of the generation were righteous, they prepared in Egypt for the geulah, by bringing with them drums and instruments for the redemption. The B'nai Yissaschar comments on the praise of the tof and the machol from tehillim 150. He wrote that the tof can be compared to the heart of a Jew. It is on the holiday of Simchat Torah, which is similar to a sealing of the heart. The first letter and the last letter of the Torah spells out the word lev (heart).

There are views that the seven hakafot are a symbolic way of removing the impediments that surround our hearts stifling the innate potential of our souls to unite with G-d's word. In addition, quoting the Maagalei Tzedek, he offers an enlightening perspective on hakafot, based on a time honored, custom. Prior to the marriage ceremony, it is customary for the bride to circle the groom seven times. This parallels the seven circuits the Jews made around Jericho when they were conquering the land from the Canaanites. The seven circuits

248

around Jericho conducted in holiness and purity destroyed the barriers of evil which enveloped the city. Similarly a bride's seven circuits around her groom during a Jewish wedding serves as a shield against the forces of impurity which defile the sanctity of marriage. The hakafot are thought to counteract any negative forces which seek to pierce the barrier and undermine the sanctity of the moment. Just as the walls of Jericho were brought down with seven circuits, so too are the walls of impurity surrounding our souls are destroyed through the seven hakafot on Simchat Torah.[1]

The Chida writes that the prayer he composed to be recited prior to the hakafos pleads with G-d 'Through the power of these hakafos, may all the impenetrable iron curtains between us and Hashem fall away.' It says in Gemara Taanis 31 that in the future Hashem will make a dance for all tzadikim.

Matisyahu Glazerson writes that the word machol was an instrument associated with dance. Others portray it as a hand drum, a tambourine cymbal or clapping. Glazerson writes that the word machol is parallel to the planet Mars and to the sphere of Gevurah (strength). The planet Mars represents war. The word milchamah war contains the letters of the word machol. War has a positive connotation; in that we are all engaged in a fight for life against the yetzer hara (the evil inclination).[2]

When a man falls into the habit of doing a certain sin it is a battle to break the habit. The struggle to atone is hinted at in the letters of the word machol, which also has the same letters as the word mechila, forgiveness. When a person chooses to repent and turn toward the right path he will be forgiven.

249

Machol also has the same root letters as the word lechem. Lechem is the gematria of 78. On Shabbos we have two portions of bread, lechem mishnah. Two times 78 is 156. This is the value of Ohel Moed, where Moshe spoke with G-d. The divine presence dwelt there (the Shechinah) The number 156 is also the value of Tzion, the place where the remains of the Temple lies today.

All life is a cycle. We connect to the Jewish year in terms of a spiral. Each time we reach a different place in time we are reaching new spiritual heights. The hakafot and the dancing reflect this spiral in time. The hakafot mark the end and the beginning as a new plateau for a new year. The circle itself is a symbol of a sacred, protected space. The circle is the shape of the earth and the moon and every other planet. Circles communicate the life force. Orbits of atoms and molecules are circular. All openings of the body are circular. In a circle there is no beginning and no end. Every day is a cyclical event. The seasons also propel us so we experience different weather systems and changes in nature.

When we gather as a group for healing or prayer it is helpful to sit in a circle. This initates a feeling of closeness. There is nothing more harmonious than to sit in a circular gathering. In our civilized world we have forgotten the messages of the circle. The circle is like the shape of the Hebrew letter Samech. The Samech is a closed round letter like a 0. The first Samech in the Torah regarding living beings appears in the narrative of the creation of Eve. Originally G-d Created male and female as one organism (Genesis1:27). However, since man has a need for a partner G-d took one of Adam's sides. The line in (Genesis 2/ 21) says Vayisgor Basar Tachtena, and he filled in (literally closed) flesh in the word vayisgor, it indicates that the woman became a separate being and is meant to provide support to the human mission in an equal fashion as man. (R.Hirsch).

A circle is a symbol of balance. The hakafot along with the cyclical completion and new beginning of the Torah readings teach us that one should avoid all extremes in all areas of life The uniqueness of an unbroken circle is that one is never at any extreme; rather he can always see himself as being in the middle point of the periphery.[3]

Another perspective on the circle relates to the soul which is the idea of gilgul neshamot or "wheel of the soul." This refers to the cycle of birth death and birth again.

The sefer Seder Hadorot explains many instances of Jewish souls that were reincarnated many times with deep explanations as to the reasons for this phenomenon.

The circle is a symbol of eternity. It goes on forever. It is eternal just as the Torah is eternal. The circle is also the symbol of equality. Every point is equidistant from its center. It is in a state of unity that the Jewish nation will again be able to live in peace again. When all Jews honor the line in Vayikra 19/18 And you should love your neighbor as yourself." This is the ultimate circle of healing. May we dance together in a circle of light, growth, unity and redemption.

Notes:

1. Simchas Torah -Art Scroll Mesorah Series by Rabbi Nosson Scherman and Rabbi Meir Zlotowitz pg 88
2. Music and Kabbalah by Rabbi Matisyahu Glazerson
3. Rambam Hilchot Deot

Made in the USA
Middletown, DE
09 September 2023

38277386R00149